Better Homes and Gardens®

CREATIVE DECORATING
on a budget

Better Homes and Gardens

CREATIVE DECORATING
on a budget

BETTER HOMES AND GARDENS BOOKS

NEW YORK   DES MOINES

Library of Congress Catalog Card Number: 72-132432

SBN: 696-00500-X

INTRODUCTION

In decorating, knowledge and imagination of the subject are vital substitutes for money. And, getting the most value from your decorating dollar is what *Better Homes and Gardens Creative Decorating on a Budget* is all about.

This heavily illustrated decorating book contains the basic elements and principles of interior design, plus hundreds of specific budget ideas. Yet, *Creative Decorating on a Budget* isn't a dream book, a wish book, or even just an idea book; it is a practical *action* book. It will teach you the how, what, and why of interior decorating—what color is, why it's important, and with specific do-it-yourself projects, how to apply it to your home. It does the same for texture, pattern, scale, balance, furniture arranging, lighting, accessories, and all the other aspects of good decorating.

Although the book is primarily composed of inexpensive do-it-yourself projects, none require more than the minimal amount of skill at wielding a paintbrush, using simple tools designed for the home handyman, or having some knowledge of basic sewing techniques. And, more importantly, each idea is adaptable and can be altered to fit *your* particular decorating budget.

After all, home is what you and your family make it, and *Better Homes and Gardens Creative Decorating on a Budget* wants to help you make it better—for less.

The Editors

Better Homes and Gardens

CONTENTS

BETTER HOMES AND GARDENS BOOKS
Editorial Director: Don Dooley
Managing Editor: Malcolm E. Robinson   Art Director: John Berg
Asst. Managing Editor: Lawrence D. Clayton   Asst. Art Director: Randall Yontz
Senior Editor: Marie Schulz
Assistant Editor: Janice McCord
Designers: Julie Zesch, Harijs Priekulis, Faith Berven

chapter 1

Establishing
A Decorating Goal

How to plan a long-range decorating goal that will help you to stretch your decorating dollar.

Contrary to popular belief, good decorating is not necessarily expensive. With practice, knowledge, and a command of the design elements—form, line, space, color, and texture—you can easily learn to decorate your home without the aid of a professional, on even the tightest of budgets. You'll be amazed by the attractive decorating results a few dollars, wisely used, can achieve. And, you'll also be amazed by how much fun you can have.

This book will provide you with the design principles and creative ideas needed to decorate your home or apartment inexpensively. As you put them into practice, you'll find your confidence increasing.

When applying any of the specific ideas found in this book, feel free to adapt, perfect, or copy any of them. Don't worry if you feel you are always repeating someone else's ideas. Remember, in decorating as in collecting works of art, a good "copy," strategically placed, can be more interesting than a poor "original."

FINDING A STARTING POINT
Remember the day you moved into your first apartment or new house and found yourself standing among the pyramids of packing crates? And, how the self-assured feeling you had enjoyed when you were "mentally" decorating the new rooms was suddenly replaced with confusion as you tried to figure out the best place to begin when creating a beautiful new home out of your old "leftovers?" The sofa was too large to go along the south wall; the furniture made the bedrooms seem even smaller; and the old draperies were too short and narrow for the living room windows.

Interior decoration, as you soon learned, is much more than clever, expensive ideas. It is the art of creating a personal environment that combines function with beauty. A beautifully decorated home doesn't just happen; it is the product of careful planning. The room pictured on the next page is the product of many years of planning, budgeting, collecting, and coordinating. Once each piece may have been used alone in another room, but now they are all combined to furnish this family room. Because the family never lost sight of its decorating goal, it was possible for the various colors, textures, patterns, and lines to coordinate to express the family's personality. You, too, can do this, even on a budget, if you know how and where to begin.

Construct a shelf of three-quarter inch ply-wood, trim with molding, and paint to make a dual-purpose display space and buffet.

ANALYZE FAMILY MEMBERS

Take a tip from the professional decorator. He wouldn't come into your home and immediately begin by selecting color schemes, furniture, and window treatments which personally appealed to him. He would spend time getting to know you, your likes and dislikes, your mode of life, and, above all, your personality.

So, begin as a professional would—on paper. Analyze each person in your family. Think of his interests, hobbies, habits, work, and personality. Give everyone a separate page in a notebook and jot down everything you can think of about him. Do this seriously and you'll have the basis for creating custom-decorated rooms. This analysis will save you the expense of a decorator and, more importantly, the cost of redoing a "not-so-successful" room which is usually the product of poor or insufficient planning.

For example, you have a seven-year-old son who builds and collects model air-planes. For this hobby and his school work, he will need a well-lighted, quiet place to study and a smooth, flat surface such as the floor or a table on which to assemble his airplanes. He will also need some type of shelves on which his collection can be stored and displayed. This suggests other factors to keep in mind: little boys and airplane glue are not compatible with fine woods, nonwashable fabrics, and most carpet fibers. Therefore, you will save both your money and your nerves if you use materials suitable to your child's needs. You might wish to use an easily maintained vinyl tile floor, durable plastic laminated furniture, and wrinkle-resist-ant, soil-resistant, washable fabrics.

Just one thought can cause a chain reaction of ideas. This will be true of every member of the family if you think carefully about his habits, hobbies, interests, and work and, more specifically, how these things affect his living environment. With this kind of planning, you will develop a decorating scheme which is unique, functional, and economical because it was specially designed to fit your family's individual needs and interests.

DO A PERSONALITY STUDY

When working on this segment of your family analysis, be honest. Sit down with your notebook and begin thinking about those characteristics which make each family member unique. For example, if your husband is the rugged outdoorsman, could you even imagine him being comfortable in a Louis XV boudoir-type living room filled with dainty, powder blue furniture and rose-satin brocade draperies? Or, a warm, outgoing person living with meek pastels and neutrals?

This is also a good time to discuss individual decorating wants with your family, including the children. Ask them what color they want for their bedrooms. After all, they are the ones who will be living in them. As you note the personal characteristics and desires of each family member, your decorating goal will begin to take on shape—a shape molded both by you and your family.

DEFINE YOUR MODE OF LIFE

The ability to see and understand peoples' individual needs is a tremendous asset when developing a decorating goal. But, the family unit as a whole must also be considered. This is particularly important when planning the decorating schemes of rooms in which the whole family entertains their guests, such as the living, dining, and family rooms.

Ask yourself questions about the activities and interests that your family shares, and jot down the answers. Do you consider your family life-style casual or formal? Do you entertain often? Is yours an active family which prefers barbecues, baseball, and the Beatles, or one that enjoys banquets, books, and Beethoven? Once again, be honest because this will save you from having to spend money on premature redecorating.

No matter which mode of living describes your family, plan your room around the activities your family enjoys.

If your idea of entertaining is having a small group of close friends over, you will undoubtedly want a warm, friendly room whose focal point is a comfortable conversation area. On the other hand, if you prefer large sit-down dinner parties, the pivotal point of your plan will be a large formal dining area that is separated from both the living room and kitchen.

After you've made your initial observations, discuss them with your family because a home that most accurately captures the spirit of the family is the result of close communication within the family itself. However, keep in mind that these long-term goals and some of your plans may not necessitate immediate action.

Think of your family life in the future as well as in its present state. If you are a young couple with no children, your situation, most probably, will be very different in a few years. You don't have to go so far as selecting colors for the nursery, but try to imagine how children will affect your decorating goals. Candlelight dining on pillows scattered around a low table may be romantic as well as practical now since you can't afford both a formal table

and the leather-tufted sofa, but begin thinking about that table anyway. Will it be a modern set of molded plastic or a traditional one of fine furniture wood?

In such a discussion, you might learn that your husband would prefer eating at least one meal a day in a formal dining room as this is where his children will learn and practice their table manners. Yet, you know that eating every meal in the dining room would be impractical. Therefore, you will want an informal dining area in the kitchen, too. Considering these ideas you may decide against buying

A room should reflect the personality and life-style of its occupants. This is achieved by color, balance, and accessories.

Bright colors make a child's room cheerful. Cover one wall with fabric or wallpaper and use its colors to coordinate the furnishings.

a dinette set until you can afford exactly what you want. Instead, compromise. Build an inexpensive breakfast bar now, and begin saving toward that wished-for dining set. The breakfast bar can be as simple or as elaborate as you wish. A board four feet long and sixteen inches wide, enameled, and supported on brackets will do the trick, or you can build a more complicated one that can be used later in the family room or den.

ANALYZE, THINK, AND PLAN
You will be amazed at how much you've already accomplished on your decorating project—and all of it on paper.

Looking back over all the facts in your notebook, you will undoubtedly see that some of your first impressions have changed and no longer seem applicable. Be thankful that you did this planning before actually ordering gallons of paint and yards of fabric. Although you may not realize it yet, careful planning has already saved you much money and, at the same time, protected you from many of the most common decorating pitfalls. Now you are on your way to a beautifully decorated home at only a fraction of the cost.

WHY YOU NEED A FLOOR PLAN
Next you come to a most important step— the floor plan. Be sure to take accurate measurements, for each succeeding step will require that these dimensions be correct. One measurement error can result in your purchasing too much wallpaper, the wrong length of draperies, or a lamp table that is too high for its chair.

Begin by taking a folding rule or long tape and measure every room. Draw a sketch of each room noting the length, width, and ceiling height. Next, draw a rough sketch of each wall indicating window and door measurements and their exact positions on the wall. Be sure to indicate on your floor plan where any breaks in the walls—recesses or projections—occur in a room. Also, indicate on the floor plan where light fixture outlets and wall electrical outlets are located in the room.

After you have completed measuring everything, the next step is to draw the floor plan to scale for your notebook. Floor plans are generally laid out on a $\frac{1}{4}$ scale because this reduces the plan to an easily workable size. For example, a 16x24 foot room drawn to $\frac{1}{4}$ scale will be only 4x6 inches in size. However, you may use any scale you wish from $\frac{1}{4}$ inch representing 1 foot to 1 inch representing 1 foot. But if you use a $\frac{1}{4}$ scale floor plan, planning your furniture arrangement will be easier because you can order the Better Homes and Gardens Furniture Arrangement Kit. This will save your drawing each piece of furniture because the kit contains 164 punch-out pieces of furniture scaled to $\frac{1}{4}$ inch equaling 1 foot. Whatever scale you decide to use, make your drawing as accurate as possible. If you don't have a scale rule, use $\frac{1}{4}$-inch squared graph paper and a ruler. From your rough sketches, transfer all measurements and dimensions to your scaled floor plan for future use.

After taking all the measurements, you are now ready to do a scale drawing of your floor plan. Use graph paper, letting one square equal one square foot. Be sure to show locations and sizes of doors, windows, and electrical outlets and fixtures. Measure, draw, and dimension accurately.

Once the room is drawn to scale, showing all the architectural features, you should take inventory of your furniture. Measure every piece for length, width, depth, and arm height. Record these measurements in your notebook. You may also draw furniture outlines to plan furniture placement.

MAKE AN INVENTORY LIST

For later reference, make a size inventory list of all your furniture. In your notebook, draw a quick sketch of each piece of furniture. Label it and note the size. For example, if your sofa is 9 feet long, note that the sofa is 108 inches long by 34 inches wide by 29 inches high. You will need to include an additional measurement for all chairs and sofas with arms. Include the arm height measurement. The arm height measurement is measured from the top of the arm to the floor.

Take the time to accurately measure every piece of furniture for length, width, and depth, and you will have completed part of the work for furniture arrangement.

START AN "IDEAS" COLLECTION

Once you have analyzed what you need, like, and want in your home, start clipping pictures and advertisements from newspapers and magazines. When reading books, magazines, pamphlets, and brochures, watch for adaptable ideas. Pay special attention to the advertising in home furnishings magazines. Many home furnishings manufacturers offer free catalogs and brochures. This is an excellent way to learn which furniture lines carry the styles you prefer. Send for this material and inquire who carries this furniture.

Make frequent visits to model homes, department stores, and furniture stores. This will enable you to see what is being done in the home furnishings field, to become acquainted with what is available, to learn how much it costs, and to know where to find the furniture.

If you are more interested in antiques, it is advisable to frequent antique shops. Chat with the dealers, letting them know what it is you are looking for. Leave your home phone number with them in case they should find something that is of particular interest to you.

A large envelope placed in the back of your notebook makes a good storage place for all your ideas. By not being permanently fixed in your notebook, it will also be easier to discard any material that no longer seems applicable or interests you.

chapter 2

Color: Mystery Or Mastery

How to save dollars by using color confidently and courageously throughout your home or apartment.

Color is your most powerful decorating tool. It is also the least expensive, easiest, and quickest tool to use to change or to create a decorating scheme. If you understand color and what it can do for you, you, too, can change the visual size and shape of a room as well as create an atmosphere and add warmth, vitality, and beauty to a room. The secret to using color successfully is to have a working knowledge of the basics of color and the courage to use this knowledge.

Color is a fun and exciting tool to use. And what's more, you don't have to be a color expert or an artist to understand it. All that's really essential is an understanding of the effects of color and then deciding exactly what you want to do with it in your decorating scheme.

In the very beginning, pinpoint exactly what you expect from your color scheme. Do you have a small room you want to appear larger or a large room you'd like to make cozier? Is there something you'd like to disguise, like an unattractive chair, a high ceiling, or an odd-sized window? Would you like to lighten your windowless bathroom or perhaps darken your bright bedroom? Do you wish your family room was more stimulating and your bedroom more soothing and restful? All of these questions are important because each poses a specific decorating problem that can be solved easily and inexpensively with something as minor as a bucket of paint, provided you know how to make the proper color selection.

Color, however, is only a part of the story. To make the most of any color scheme, the added interest achieved by the use of texture and pattern is also essential. Texture is softness, smoothness, hardness, and roughness. It is the surface feel of three-dimensional objects. Pattern is really a visual texture. It can be seen but not felt. For example, the room at right is unquestionably colorful and would remain so even if you chose to replace the striped sofa with a solid yellow one. But the interest created by that one element of pattern, a visual texture, would be lost. As you can see, color, texture, and pattern are dependent on one another, so to master the mystery of color, you must also understand pattern and texture. Basic concepts, yes, but they are essential.

the plastic elements: color, texture, and pattern

The plastic elements—color, texture, and pattern—are the elements of design that give size, shape, and dimension to everything around us. To use them effectively, you should understand their effects.

Hue refers to a particular name of a color, like red or blue. And, every hue has two dimensions, value and intensity. *Value* has to do with a color's lightness or darkness. As colors are mixed with white or black, their values change. Those mixed with white are called tints and have higher values than do shades that have been mixed with black. *Intensity* or tone refers to the brightness or dullness of a color. By adding gray—a mixture of black and white to any color, you lower the intensity and it becomes more dull and muted.

There are a number of systems used to classify colors, but the one most commonly used is a color wheel based on three primary colors—red, yellow, and blue—which exist without mixing. There are also three secondary colors—orange, violet, and green—which are created by mixing equal parts of one primary with another. Mixing red with yellow in equal proportions makes orange, blue with red makes

Borrow a color scheme from an expert, an artist. This complementary scheme using the primary colors, red, yellow, and blue with white was developed from the room's focal point, a painting.

violet, and yellow plus blue makes green. By mixing each primary color with its neighboring secondary color, you get the intermediate colors. There are six of these —yellow-orange, red-orange, red-violet, blue-violet, blue-green, and yellow-green. This mixing of colors can go on indefinitely, producing thousands of colors just waiting for you to coordinate them.

The combination of two or more of these hues results in a color scheme. Although there are very few hard and fast rules regarding color, there are several formalized color schemes that can be classified into two major groups—related and contrast-

ing color schemes. Related color schemes are based on common hues and tend to create restful, quiet effects. Monochromatic and analogous schemes are the two types of related schemes. Contrasting color schemes are based on opposing hues and tend to be stimulating and balanced because they include both warm and cool hues. There are five contrasting color schemes; simple complementary, double-complementary, split-complementary, tetrad, and triad. You can build any one or all of these schemes if you work with a color wheel and understand the components of each scheme.

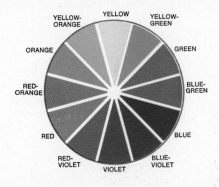

The color wheel contains three groups of colors: primary—red, yellow, and blue; secondary—orange, green, and violet, and tertiary—colors achieved by mixing primary and secondary colors with their neighbors.

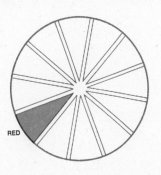

Monochromatic schemes are related schemes using only one color in a wide range of value and intensity. This base color and two variations plus a neutral create a good background for accessories and art objects.

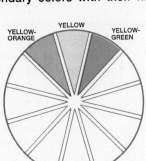

Analogous schemes are related schemes, but they consist of three or more colors which are near or adjacent one another on the color wheel or which have a common hue. This scheme's common hue is yellow.

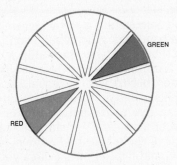

A simple complementary scheme is composed of any two hues directly opposite each other on the color wheel. Using this scheme, every room will have both warm and cool colors, but one hue must dominate.

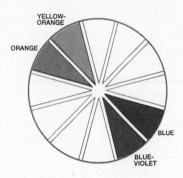

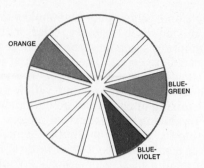

Double complementary color schemes have four colors and, are more difficult to work with. They consist of any two adjacent hues and their respective complements—the hues directly opposite them on the wheel.

Split-complementary schemes consist of any hue and the two hues on each side of its complement—the opposite color. If you use orange, its complement is blue, so you also use blue-green and blue-violet.

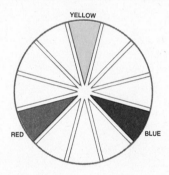

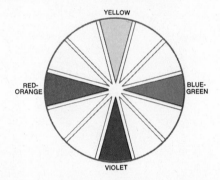

Triad schemes are made of any three hues that are equidistant from each other on the color wheel. Here, the primary colors are used. Remember to select a dominate hue and keep the others subordinate to it.

Tetrad schemes are based on any four hues that are equidistant from one another on the color wheel. This scheme works best if you use one color in large amounts and the others as accent colors.

To be successful, a color scheme must please you and your family and, at the same time, must be practically suited to your room and its uses. Naturally, your selection begins with personal taste. But the scheme should also contain hues that you can live with comfortably for a long period of time. Also consider the physical aspects of the room—its function, size, exposure, and lighting. The colors you select and, in part, the color scheme's success depend on these factors.

In your beginning efforts at building a color scheme, it's better to limit yourself to three or four colors. Choose one color as a starting point, and after deciding which of the seven possible schemes best suits your needs, select several companion colors for the major hue by using the color wheel and the definition of your chosen color scheme.

Since the walls constitute the largest area of color in a room, you will find it easier to coordinate a color scheme if you choose this color first. For large areas, quiet colors are easier to live with than are bolder ones. The color used for large upholstered pieces and draperies can be brighter and bolder. But, reserve the brightest, boldest color for the decorative accessories, which make up only a small percentage of the room's total color ratio.

By using the accent color of one room as the major color of the next room, one scheme can be used throughout the house.

There are several ways to build a color scheme. Starting with your favorite color and a color wheel, you can build any scheme. Or, single out the colors used in a favorite painting or fabric you've already planned to use. But the method most often used is that of imitating a color scheme used in a model display room or pictures from a book or magazine.

If you want to adapt a color scheme, first analyze all the components of the scheme—color, texture, and pattern. List the colors you find and note how each is used—as major, minor, or accent elements. Note the value and intensity of each color used and decide which color dominates in the particular color scheme.

Next, make a list of all the pattern used in the room. List the type of pattern (bold or subdued), the color combination used, where the pattern is used (floors, walls, ceilings, or furniture), and the proportion of pattern to solid.

To ensure against overlooking even the most subtle textural contribution, list the sources of texture used in your model room, from sparkling glass and shiny metal to nubby fabric and carpeting to rough stone and brick.

After making a checklist noting the colors, textures, patterns, balance, and proportion used in the model scheme, you can transpose this scheme to any room. Using quick sketches or a floor plan and colored furniture cutouts, try different variations. Try the major color on the floor, then on the upholstered pieces. Do the same with the pattern. Try it in the draperies, then on the wall. Keep experimenting until you find exactly what you want or you'll never know what exciting possibilities you may have missed!

When choosing a color scheme for a room that is primarily wood toned, keep in mind that wood tones are colors—either warm or cool—and must, therefore, be considered as part of the scheme.

put color to work for you

Create a more spacious feeling with color. It's easy to do if you remember the effects of color: light, cool, colors recede and make any object appear larger. Bright, cool colors advance, if strongly contrasted with the background, but will appear smaller than objects using bright, warm colors.

Large scaled, patterned furniture requires space. Push back the walls and increase the size of any room by painting the walls white or a light, cool color.

Raise the temperature in any chilly, no sunshine room simply by changing the color scheme. Create your own sunshine. Choose sun colors—red, yellow, and orange—from the warm side of the color wheel.

Develop an analogous scheme using at least three related colors in the red, red-orange, orange, yellow-orange, and yellow group. Allow one color to dominate and use it full strength on large areas. Paint one wall with a bold, warm color to shrink the size of the room. This will create the warm, cozy atmosphere you desire.

Just knowing the basic components of color schemes and how to assemble them is not enough. In order to make the most of the "magical powers" of color, you must know what color can do for your home.

Color's power goes further than reflecting one's personality; it can deceive the eye as well. For example, if you need a larger, lighter room, make the walls recede by using white or tints of the cooler hues—blue, green, and violet. Thinking on a slightly larger scale, use this principle to increase the apparent size of a small apartment. Instead of creating a dramatic effect in each room using a different scheme, devise a cool, receding color scheme using no more than three hues. Repeat this scheme throughout the apartment, varying the color proportions and you can create a feeling of flow that allows you to move from room to room unaware of walls.

However, using the bold, warm hues of red, yellow, and orange has the opposite effect. They make walls advance and therefore, the room will appear smaller.

For example, try painting a short wall of a rectangular room a sunny yellow and notice how the short walls advance and the room appears to be more square.

Color also can change the apparent temperature of a room. A room with a northern exposure rarely gets the sun and may seem chilly. Paint it a warm, tropical orange and watch the temperature and comfort levels rise.

In addition to changing the visual size and shape of a room and its apparent temperature, color can help conceal or emphasize a room's architectural features or furnishings. You can conceal an ugly chair by covering it in a color that matches or closely blends with the wall. Or, emphasize an attractive chair by projecting it with a contrasting color.

Once you have all of the color principles well in mind, you can make the most of every decorating dollar because you are in complete command of the most powerful, yet inexpensive decorating element of all—color. Here are a few more rules regarding the use of color that you will want to keep in mind for future use.

Color can even create a new mood in your home, and it is much less costly than replacing furniture and accessories.

1. Bold, warm colors advance.
2. Light, cool colors recede.
3. Avoid using more than one pattern in a room.
4. Use cool colors—blues, greens, and purples—in rooms that are too sunny.
5. Use warm colors—reds, yellows, and oranges—in dull, dark, gloomy rooms.
6. Unequal areas of color provide more interest. Plan to use your major color in two-thirds of the room.
7. Color is affected by its neighbors. Put color swatches together before making final choices.
8. Color is affected by light. Test colors in both natural and artificial light before purchasing them.

Attractive furniture will stand out with contrast if it isn't forced to compete or blend with its surroundings.

chapter 3

Acquiring Furniture

A furniture purchase can be a permanent investment if you know how it will be used today and tomorrow.

Good buymanship is more than having money to spend. It also includes knowing what you want, where to find it, and what to do with the piece once you get it home.

The amount of money you have to spend doesn't determine whether or not your decorating results will be successful. True, it takes money to buy anything, but the real key to wise buymanship is how you spend rather than how much you spend.

For example, one married couple had waited years to purchase their dream, a king-sized bed. They bought traditionally styled, quality furniture and in less than a year were transferred to another area. Because the house they purchased had small bedrooms, they had to sell their "over-sized" dream at a considerable loss.

A similarly sad story involves another couple—a young couple faced with an empty apartment, and a limited budget. They financed the bare essentials from a so-called "economy" line to make do until they could afford what they wanted. Four years, two children, and numerous additional bills later, they found that the finance payments were going to outlive the furniture which would soon have to be replaced by still more "economy" pieces.

These are very common mistakes. The first couple knew what they wanted and apparently where to find it but didn't plan for its future use. The second couple had a good idea of what they wanted but settled for quantity rather than quality. It would have been wiser had they purchased a few quality-line pieces of their chosen style, or selected the same style in a less expensive, but still quality line.

GOOD INVESTMENTS MEAN SAVINGS

The most economical way to acquire furniture is to consider each purchase a permanent investment. A little thoughtful planning is the key—knowing exactly what you want for both now and for the future. If you are just getting started, concentrate on the necessities. The room shown at the right was treated this way. The first purchases were the essential pieces, in a timeless, tireless style. Then with time, money, and experience, the accessories were added to complete the room's decor. Also remember, if in your future you plan to include children, select durable furniture and soil-resistant, sturdy fabrics in dark colors rather than fragile, delicate

pieces of furniture, accessories, and fabric.

For example, suppose you had invested nearly all of your household budget in a really smashing sofa when you were first married. Then you purchased two woven rattan basket chairs for twenty dollars each to complete the living room's seating requirement. Sixteen years later, the *newly re-upholstered* sofa is in the family room and the woven rattan basket chairs are in use on the sun porch. A sentimental approach true, but a practical one. Not a single penny wasted in replacing furniture, and no money lost by having to sell or haul away unwanted furniture. Each piece is as functional and attractive today as it was the day it was purchased. But, for this method of acquiring furniture to be successful, you first must decide on a furniture style, one you will like day after day.

SELECT A FURNITURE STYLE

When selecting a furniture style, let the general atmosphere or mood you wish to create in your home be your guide. Do you want the country-casual look, the stark-contemporary look, or the more formal look of a French-period style?

Whichever look, atmosphere, or mood you prefer, an intelligent selection of a particular furniture style depends on your knowledge of furniture styles in general. You don't have to be a walking encyclopedia of furniture styles; you simply have to be informed enough to distinguish English styles from Spanish styles. This knowledge is easily attainable with a little work and patience on your part.

You can begin by taking a special interest in style. After a short time, you will begin to prefer one particular style. Assume that

Eclecticism—a marriage of the old with the new, the past with the present, and the native with the foreign. It is a challenging treatment that immediately expresses the owner's personality.

you want to use something English. As this style covers many centuries, you will need to narrow your search to a specific period. Go to museums, showrooms, and libraries studying the one style that best fits your family's mode of life.

Generally, furniture styles are divided into three classifications: traditional, provincial, and contemporary. Traditional styles are those which were favored by rulers and by wealthy patrons of the top cabinetmakers of the day. These styles were named after a reigning power or a master craftsman and include Chippendale, Hepplewhite, Georgian, Louis XIV-XVI, Sheraton, William and Mary, and Queen Anne styles.

Provincial styles, although less ornate and sophisticated, are descendants of the traditional styles. These styles are named after the geographic location from which they came and include American colonial, American, French and Italian provincial, Pennsylvania Dutch, and Shaker. The difference in style resulted from the local cabinetmaker's limited skill and tools. In many cases provincial styles were interpretations or copies of the traditional.

Contemporary styles do not describe a period but rather a continual process of development. Style lines and characteristics change with each designer's influence and inspiration. Contemporary styles reflect what is currently fashionable—Mediterranean, Early American, modern, Oriental, Scandinavian, traditional, or Shaker.

DECIDE ON A TREATMENT

Once you've chosen a style, decide how it is going to be treated in your long-range decorating goal. To guide you there are three classifications of treatments: purist, suggestive, and eclectic. Simply decide which is more practical for you.

The purist treatment requires that everything from furniture and accessories to color schemes be authentically from one period. This treatment requires extensive research and money and often results in a room with a museumlike atmosphere. For example, following the purist theory, a room done in the Queen Anne

Just a few pieces can express a period. Cabriole legs, shell motifs, and oriental rugs will reflect the Queen Anne period.

style is comprised of things strictly from that period of English history.

If, instead, you prefer to use the Queen Anne style with a suggestive treatment, you could use the primary pieces of furniture from the Queen Anne style. But the window, wall, and floor treatments and accessories could be from any style, period, or country as long as you continue the feeling or atmosphere by remaining consistent.

Perhaps you prefer the eclectic treatment which combines two or more distinct styles. This is the most economical treat-

Soft pastel colors, painted and gilded surfaces, and shaped cabriole legs combine to create this fragile, feminine, and definitely French dining room which features both Louis XV and XVI styles.

ment. An example of this would be period pieces combined with ultramodern furniture. A modern sofa and lacquered T-squared table might be used successfully with a Victorian Bentwood rocker, an oriental rug, and accessories from India.

No matter what period or treatment you decide upon, keep in mind that it is entirely possible to have a "period" look using very few pieces of furniture from that period. Create a feeling for the period by using the period's color schemes, wall treatments, and accessories. This will be invaluable for families who are just establishing their decorating goals. Make do with the furniture you now have but create the mood immediately. You can have the look you want without waiting until you can afford more furniture. Simply buy the accompanying furniture whenever it is most convenient for you.

HOW TO BUY CASE PIECES

Every furniture shopper wants to get the most for his money. This demands a wise and sometimes shrewd buyer—a person who knows reputable dealers and manufacturers, the qualities of woods and finishes, the guidelines of good construction, and what things should cost. All of this information is easily attainable in showrooms and furniture stores as well as in manufacturers' brochures.

Construction is the prime ingredient of durability. Know that when a piece is labeled "solid" walnut, it means the piece is made entirely of walnut. Or, if the tag reads "genuine" mahogany, it

Mediterranean styles have enjoyed wide-spread popularity. This style favors the lavish use of rich color, abstract patterns, sculptured turnings, and deep moldings. They create a masculine feeling that blends easily with other contemporary styles.

Authentic antiques, reproductions, and contemporary pieces successfully combine to create this warm American colonial room. This style alone makes up one-fourth of all the furniture sold.

means the structural parts are of solid mahogany and the flat surfaces of veneered mahogany. Do not be confused by the term "veneer." It does not mean poor or cheap construction as it did several years ago when an animal-base glue was used.

Today, most furniture is veneered, and because of a better synthetic resin which provides a more secure bond, veneer's reputation has improved greatly. Because of its sandwiched construction, a veneered piece defies warping, is strong and offers a greater variety of both grain and pattern than does that of solid construction.

Also, know the characteristics of the principal woods. *Ash*, used primarily in frames and unexposed parts, is strong, hard, and durable. *Birch*, used in the structural parts, is strong, fine grained,

and relatively inexpensive. *Cherry*, the most widely used fruitwood, is light, strong, rather hard, and expensive. *Mahogany* is a favorite of craftsman because of its hardness, variety of grain, and workability. *Maple* is hard, dense, and shapes easily, and is highly resistant to splitting. *Oak*, a sturdy wood, is durable and well suited to carving and special finishes. *Pecan* is often used for solid, exposed parts because it is very heavy, dense, and strong. *Pine* is a soft, light wood that is easily dented. *Walnut*, the most popular furniture wood today, is hard, but easily worked, resistant to warping, and offers a great variety of grain.

When shopping for furniture, pay special attention to the joints because they give strength and long life to a piece of furniture. These indicators of quality should be tight and smooth and should fit perfectly without the assistance of plastic wood filler. Also, see how the glue is applied to the joints. If it is done sloppily, quality has been sacrificed. The use of screws rather than nails for reinforcement and joining is another sign of poor quality.

Finishes are also vitally important and one of the easiest ways a manufacturer can skimp. A finish is applied to protect and enhance the beauty of wood. A hand-rubbed oil finish is used on most quality furniture. It is a good natural protector and makes most scratches self-healing. Water spots are easily repaired, and an oil finish will never craze or crack as will

a shellac, varnish, paint, or lacquer finish which produces a harder but more diffi-cult-to-repair finish.

Other quality guidelines for case piece furniture include:

1. The piece should be level and rigid. It should not wobble under pressure.
2. All unexposed parts should be sanded smooth and stained to match the rest of the piece.
3. All movable parts should fit well and operate easily.
4. Drawers should include drawer stops, drawer glides, and dust panels.
5. The stain and finish should be applied smoothly and evenly.
6. Hardware should be solid and heavy.

elements of quality construction

The backs of chests should be screwed to frames and supported and fastened along the bottom for additional strength. In better-qual-ity furniture, the backs are also well sanded, stained, and waxed.

Remove a couple of drawers and look at the inside construction. Quality pieces have friction-free center drawer guides and drawer stops to keep them lined up prop-erly, and protective dust panels.

Drawers should be constructed with accurately cut, well-fitted dovetail joints. Pull the drawer out halfway and move it from side to side. There shouldn't be more than ¼ inch of play on either side of the drawer.

Look for interior finishing. The in-side of the piece of furniture won't be as finished as the outside, but it should at least be sanded smooth, stained, and waxed. Also, be sure to examine how the hard-ware is attached.

HOW TO BUY UPHOLSTERED FURNITURE

The old saying, "You can't tell a book by its cover," is certainly applicable when shopping for upholstered furniture. As a great many of the quality check points lie under the surface, it is extremely important that you buy "name" brands from reputable dealers. Ask them questions, read the tags, and look for the National Association of Furniture Manufacturers' "Seal of Integrity."

In order to ask knowledgeable questions, you should know what constitutes quality upholstered goods and how they are made.

The frame comes first and is made of strong, dense, hardwoods such as oak, birch, elm, and poplar. The joints should be either mortise-and-tenon or double-dowel to withstand the stress and strain of daily use. Corner blocks should also be used to reinforce the legs.

Next, tightly woven bands of jute are interlaced and securely tacked to the frame. Highly tempered, enameled steel springs should be anchored to the webbing. Twelve springs per seat is the best and eight, the minimum. To keep the springs in place and to prevent sagging, proper tying is essential. In better-quality furniture, each spring is tied eight times in four directions with hemp or flax twine.

The filling process comes next. On the front edge of the seats a special reinforcement of rolled burlap or cellulose is applied. This edging provides better structure for the seats. Directly over the springs, a covering of burlap or cotton felt is applied to anchor the springs and provide a solid base for the filling. Horsehair is the best filling. But, kapok, palm fiber, and sisal are also used in combination with the hair. Foam rubber is rapidly becoming a popular filling in the medium to high-priced ranges because it is comfortable, durable, resilient, and strong. Over the filling is a layer of cotton, a layer of muslin, and finally the upholstery fabric.

Today's modern style is characterized by clean, simple lines, geometric forms, and the elimination of ornament for ornament's sake. It expresses new materials, new methods, and a new honesty.

Upholstery fabric must be strong and resistant to abrasion. The most durable fabrics are heavy and closely woven with few threads that can pull or catch. Test the fabric by pulling it both crosswise and lengthwise to see if the threads shift. Also, scratch the fabric to see if it snags.

The fiber content of upholstery material is only one part of the fabric story. The new protective fabric finishes should also be considered. Many upholstery fabrics come treated with special finishes to make them waterproof, soil resistant, stain resistant, and wrinkle resistant. These finishes make upholstered pieces more durable and easier to care for.

Read the tags to see if the fabric has been treated. If it has not and you desire it to be, you can have it treated by a finisher or do it yourself with the spray-on stain repellents which are now available.

By following these guides, reading and understanding the information on the tags, and shopping for "name" brands from reputable dealers, you will be able to purchase upholstered furniture that will last a lifetime. However, don't overlook one very important element—comfort. Sit on the chair or sofa. Notice the angle of the back, the depth and height of the seat, and height of the arms, and the firmness of the cushions. Unless the upholstered piece is comfortable and, therefore, serviceable, you will find yourself hoping it can soon be replaced!

HOW TO BUY ANTIQUES

Whether collecting authentic antiques or renovating attic stowaways, nearly everyone has been caught up in the "antique" craze. Antique shops have popped up everywhere overnight, and operating them are instant authorities on antiques.

Unless you're certain you are dealing with a reputable dealer, it will be to your advantage financially to be an authority yourself. Know the furniture periods, particularly which woods are characteristic of which period. Know the woods and finishes. If you are able to recognize the color and grain of various woods, you will never buy what appears to be a solid walnut, hand-oiled Empire chest, only to find that it is actually a mass-produced pine reproduction covered with a few coats of walnut stain and shellac.

Also, know approximately what things are worth. This will come naturally as you shop around. But, don't take the price tag at face value. Antique shop prices are not always firm. The prices marked are often the starting prices. It will be to your advantage to bargain with the dealer as the marked price is often about twenty-five percent over what he will actually take.

To evaluate the worth of something, you must know what constitutes bad condition and how much work, time, and money it will take to restore the piece. Use the same check points you would if you were buying a new piece of quality furniture. If you are buying an upholstered piece, know approximately how much it will cost to have it reupholstered. You may find that it really isn't such a bargain.

Authentic antiques, anything made prior to 1830, in good or repairable condition, are always good investments because they can usually be sold for a profit, particularly if you purchased them in the rough and restored them yourself. They are like money in the bank. Take, for example, the Tiffany hanging lampshade of the Victorian era. These aren't 140 years old yet, but they made their comeback in 1957-58 at which time they could have been purchased for a few dollars. Today, these same leaded, jewel-tone glass shades are a valued collector's item.

Acquiring antique furniture, authentic or otherwise, through shops, auctions, or newspaper advertisements, can be a fun and economical way to "collect" furniture. You might buy one really good piece and build a room around it. Or, you might want to buy an inexpensive, unusual storage cabinet that, with a lot of work, will make a great conversation piece. There are innumerable budget-stretching possibilities for the imaginative. Just be certain you know what you're buying, its restoration cost and time, and what you're going to do with it both now and in your future decorating plans.

guidelines for identifying furniture style

	Identifying Characteristics	Dominant Woods	Colors
Louis XV 1723-1774	Small, dainty, graceful. Free-flowing "S" curves. Upholstered pads on chair arms. Gilded caning. Chinese lacquer. Motifs—wreaths, flowers, ribbons, shells, and cupids.	Oak, mahogany, walnut, beech, ebony, rosewood.	Rose, dove gray, silver, gold, powder blue, light green.
Louis XVI 1774-1793	Small, simple, rectangular forms. Legs—straight, tapered, fluted. Subdued lacquer; some inlay. Motifs—lyres, oak leaf, torches, garlands. Strong Greek, Roman, and Egyptian influence.	Mahogany, beech, walnut, rosewood, satinwood.	Either muted or strong. White, gold, green, pink, blue, crimson.
Queen Anne 1702-1714	Graceful, curved line. Legs—cabriole, "S" curve, claw feet. Beauty of wood—carving, veneer. Very little ornamentation. Motif—scalloped shell.	Walnut Cherry	Soft crimson, blues, greens, deep yellows.
Chippendale 1754-1779	Solid graceful forms. Chinese influence. Much carving, fretwork, and grooving in scrolls. Legs—Chinese or cabriole with claw and ball feet. Motifs—shell, ribbon, pagoda, lattice.	Mahogany Some Chinese pieces lacquered.	Rich, muted reds, greens, turquoise, yellows.
English Georgian 1760-1806	Designs of Adam Brothers. Hepplewhite, Sheraton. Graceful, dainty, carving, inlay, spade feet. Legs—straight, tapered, round, fluted. Motifs—plumes, wreaths, lyres, swags.	Mahogany Satinwood Exotic veneers	Soft blues, greens, grays, yellows, roses.
Early American 1607-1700	Crude undecorated adaptation of English styles-Jacobean and William and Mary. Simple, straight lines. Rush seats. Ladder and banister chair backs. Turned spindle legs.	Pine, maple, cherry, oak.	Warm reds, blues, greens, yellows, and browns against mellow wood tones.
American Colonial 1700-1781	Adaptation of Queen Anne, Georgian, and Chippendale styles. Spindle backed. Windsor chair, rocking chair. Block-front furniture.	Mahogany, walnut, pine, maple.	White, cream, blue gray, mustard, reds, greens, browns.
Federal/ Empire 1781-1825	Refined, graceful lines inspired by Adam, Sheration, Hepplewhite. Veneering, spool furniture. Unadorned wooden pulls. Motifs—eagles, lyres, swags, stars.	Mahogany Cherry	Soft to rich reds, blues, greens, yellows, browns.
Victorian 1825-1900	Overly ornate curves and ornamentation, heavy carving. Marble table tops. Suites of furniture used caned and bentwood chairs. Motifs—scrolls, foliage, grapes.	Black walnut, red mahogany rosewood, oak, cherry.	Deep reds, maroons, greens, blues, and browns.
French Provincial	Simplified versions of Louis XIII-XVI. Emphasized beauty of wood. Natural wax finish. Avoided gilt, paint, and marquetry. Simple carved ornamentation. Legs—straight or cabriole.	Walnut, chestnut, oak, fruitwoods.	Soft rose, dove gray, silver, powder blue, light green.
Italian Provincial	Large scale. Eliminated lavish ornamentation. Rectangular forms. Legs—straight, square, tapered. Outline molding. Finish—paint or lacquer. Brass hardware.	Walnut, mahogany, and fruitwood.	Deep reds, maroons, blues, greens, and golds.

and coordinating period room settings

Wall Treatments	Floor Coverings	Fabrics	Accessories	Related Styles
Decorated wood panels. Chinese wallpaper.	Parquet floors. Aubuson and Oriental rugs in delicate colors.	Brocades, silks, satins, damasks, printed cottons, taffeta, and velvets.	Mirrors. Porcelain. Chinese art objects. Silver candlesticks.	Louis XIII Louis XIV Italian Renaissance Georgian Chippendale
Decorated panels. Paint, paper, fabric, mirror.	Parquet floors. Oriental and French rugs.	Cottons, silks, taffeta, satin. Striped floral and feather designs.	Nymphs. Satyrs. Statuettes. Oil lamps.	Adam Sheraton Hepplewhite Directoire styles
Painted wood panels. Wallpaper Printed fabric	Oriental, Aubusson, needlepoint rugs.	Damasks, velvets, linen chintz with small foliage and flower designs.	Tall clocks. Boxes. Chinese porcelain. Fire screens. Brass and crystal chandeliers.	William and Mary Chippendale Georgian American Colonial
Painted Papered Paneled	Oriental French Domestic (figured)	Printed linens, damasks, chintz, antique satins.	Elaborate clocks. Brass candlesticks. Chinese pottery. Pier glasses. Lanterns.	American Colonial Louis XV Queen Anne Georgian Contemporary styles
Plastered Painted Papered Paneled	Oriental French Domestic (figured)	Brocade, damask, satin, taffeta	Clocks. Mirrors. Porcelain plaques. Candlesticks. Vases. Chinese objects d'art.	Louis XVI Empire Directoire Colonial
Paneled Painted	Braided, hooked, and homespun rugs.	Buckram, chintz, muslin, linen, crewel, calicos, ginghams.	Pewter cups and candlesticks. Copper cooking utensils. Lanterns. Bible boxes. Wrought iron.	William and Mary Jacobean American Colonial Duncan Phyfe Shaker
Paneled Painted Papered	Oriental and French rugs popular in city. Hooked and braided in country.	Chintz, muslin, damask, brocade, linen, leather.	Country—used Early American. City—more refined-Brass. Silver. Clocks. Mirrors. Porcelain.	Queen Anne Georgian Chippendale Italian Provincial 18th century styles
Fabric Paneled Papered Painted	Hooked and Oriental rugs.	Damasks, chintz, velvets, brocades, needlepoint.	Clocks. Sheraton mirrors. Paintings. Etchings. Brass candlesticks. Scones. Cut glass vases. Brass and crystal chandeliers.	Georgian Chippendale French Empire French Directoire
Painted Fabric Paper (large floral patterns)	Axminster and Brussels carpets.	Velours, velvets, tapestries. (fringe, braid, and tassel trim.)	Large pier glasses. Porcelain figurines. Molded cut glass. Antimacassars. Silver-plated pieces. Shades for oil lamps. Palms ferns.	Queen Anne William and Mary American Colonial Modern
Paneled Painted Fabric Papered	Reed Oriental and Domestic rugs. (figured)	Toile, damasks, muslins, brocades.	Mirrors. Porcelain. Chinese art objects. Silver candlesticks.	American Colonial Victorian Italian Provincial Other 18th century styles. Modern
Paneled Painted Fabric Papered	Carpeting Reed Oriental (figured)	Toile, damasks, muslins, brocades.	Paintings. Urns. Vases. Sconces. Marble. Colored glass.	French Provincial American Colonial Modern Other formal 18th century styles.

chapter 4

Furniture Arranging

How to create low-cost furniture arrangements that will provide maximum service, beauty, and versatility.

Careful furniture arrangements can improve poor architectural features, emphasize good ones, reroute traffic, and create centers of interest where none previously existed. Therefore, planning good furniture arrangements is essential to your success at furniture arranging.

If you use your head instead of your husband's back, arranging furniture need not be a tiring, time-consuming game of musical chairs. Let the room's purpose guide your planning. Today, most rooms must be multipurpose. So when planning, decide what activities you will perform in each room. For example, bedrooms are used primarily for sleeping and dressing. Therefore, arrange bedroom furniture to achieve maximum comfort, convenience, and use of space. To do this, place the bed along the wall opposite the entrance. This way you won't be walking around the bed every time you enter the room to get something from the dresser.

Next, develop your plan on paper using the scaled floor plan and furniture size inventory list in your notebook. Using only the length and width measurements, draw on graph paper and cut out the scaled furniture shapes or purchase the Better Homes & Gardens Furniture Arrangement Kit mentioned on page 10. Color the cutouts to indicate the furniture's color.

Now, lightly sketch arrows on the floor plan to show traffic patterns (the obvious paths people take to enter and exit a room). By defining these paths in the beginning, you will avoid placing furniture where it will disrupt traffic.

Next, determine your focal point. It may be an architectural focal point such as a fireplace or window wall, or it may be an unusual piece of furniture, an area rug, or a wall of art. No matter what it is, build your furniture arrangement around this magnetic point. For example, the room at right has no architectural focal point. So, the patterned sofa is arranged on the longest wall, flanked by tall cabinets, and further emphasized by colorful accessories. The furniture grouping now becomes the room's focal point and dictates the placement of all other pieces of furniture.

When the initial planning is finished, arrange and rearrange the paper cutouts on the floor plan until you have the grouping that is most suitable. Then actually move the furniture into place. As you will see, using paper cutouts saves much work.

elements to consider

Planning a working furniture arrangement requires a careful eye for judging size, shape, scale, and balance. These elements are rarely given much thought, but they are not automatic and do require particular attention when arranging furniture.

Scale is the proportion of one object in relation to its surroundings. This means the size of the room, its furnishings, and the people using the furnishings should all be related. For example, a small room will appear larger when small-scaled furniture is used instead of large-scaled furniture.

Scale, as it applies to the size and shape of furniture within a room, is often misused because it is difficult to visualize how a piece of furniture in a showroom will look in a normal-sized room. The best advice to follow is to think "small."

In interior design there are two types of balance to consider: formal or symmetrical, and informal or asymmetrical. Whichever type you choose to use depends on the atmosphere you wish to create.

Formal balance is achieved when all objects on one side of a central line are repeated on the opposite side. This means one side will be the mirror image of the other. It's an easy effect to achieve but can become quite monotonous.

Informal balance tends to be more stimulating. It is achieved when equal but unidentical objects are balanced on each side of a center point.

The total concept of balance includes size and shape relationships as well as the balance of light, color, and texture as discussed in chapters 2 and 8.

In the room below, a symmetrical arrangement of large, but properly scaled furniture pieces is centered around the room's focal point, the window wall with its picturesque scenery.

Small rooms needn't be cramped or uninteresting. By aligning small-scaled furniture along the walls, you can put every inch of space to use. What you lack in floor space, make up for on walls. Here, bright, contrasting colors and tasteful accessories informally arranged create a magnetic center of interest.

basic arrangement ideas...

Very few rooms in homes or apartments are "ideal." So, make the best of the situation by using your knowledge of furniture arrangement and your imagination to camouflage the flaws.

Square rooms generally seem smaller than they are and, therefore, should be treated the same as small rooms. (Place furniture parallel to the walls to avoid breaking up the space.) Use small-scaled, light furniture to conserve floor space. Lengthen the room by building a strong horizontal line of long, low cabinets or bookcases. And, push back the walls with a light, cool, solid-colored background.

If you aren't fond of bowling alleys or gymnasiums, large or long rooms should be visually shortened. To do this, concentrate on the short wall farthest from the entrance. A bold pattern, a bright color, a large vertical piece of furniture, or anything eye-catching placed on this wall will make it appear closer. Dividing the room into areas of specific activity by placing a sofa, table, desk, or pair of chairs at right angles to one of the long walls will also help to shorten the room. Because this will interrupt the flow of space, pay careful attention to the location of traffic patterns. Avoid bisecting these patterns.

Overcome the confining feeling of small, boxlike rooms by expanding the space with wall and window treatments in receding colors and small-scaled furniture you can see through as well as under.

The solution to the furniture arrangement problem in this long, narrow room was to conserve space by aligning furniture with the walls and to visually widen it by emphasizing the horizontal line.

BASIC RULES TO FOLLOW

The most important qualities of good furniture arrangement are comfort and convenience. To ensure these qualities, observe the following basic rules regarding spacial dimensions and furniture positioning:

1. In a conversation area, arrange seating so that people can converse easily, with chairs no more than eight feet apart. Avoid straight-line arrangements which do not allow for good eye contact.

2. Always arrange furniture so it may be used conveniently. An end table that is just out of reach is useless.

3. If you use a coffee table in front of a sofa, allow 14 to 18 inches of space between the two pieces of furniture.

4. Use the proper table height if you want maximum use, efficiency, and beauty, particularly if used in conjunction with lamps. Coffee tables should be the same height as the sofa cushions. Other tables should be the same height as the arm height of any adjacent chair.

5. In a kitchen or dining room, allow at least 54 inches of space between the chair and wall to provide ample space for seating and serving.

6. When making furniture arrangements, remember that traffic lanes should be at least 30 inches wide.

7. Avoid arranging any piece of furniture crosswise in a corner.

Try to keep in mind that an over-furnished room often looks cramped and confusing, while a more sparsely furnished room appears spacious and refreshing. So the best rule to follow when decorating is —when in doubt, leave it out. Most decorators follow this same advice.

space-stretching ideas...
dual-purpose furniture

"Two for the price of one" is a welcome phrase to every economy-minded person. It means stretching dollars, saving pennies, and getting the most for your money. This phrase is also a perfect description of dual- or multipurpose furniture.

Each piece of this furniture does at least two jobs. It is furniture that folds down, pulls out, flips over, or moves around to serve another purpose. The oldest and probably most well-known type of dual-purpose furniture is the sleeper-sofa, a sofa that turns into a full-sized bed. It takes very little space when folded up, provides comfortable seating by day, and guest sleeping space by night. And, it allows the room to function as both a living room and as an extra bedroom. Therefore, dual-purpose furniture can transform any room into a multipurpose room that will more adequately fulfill your family's needs through the most efficient use of space.

There are many examples of dual-purpose furniture on the market today—dining tables that masquerade as desks, china hutches, and storage cabinets when not in use; benches and tables that camouflage storage spaces; and chests that unfold to reveal buffet servers and bars. Available in almost every style, these pieces are beautifully designed, extremely functional, and remarkably efficient.

If money is at a premium in your decorating scheme, put dual-purpose furni-

Dual-purpose furniture means double savings for you. Although you'll probably use it as a coffee table most of the time, it can also be raised to dining table height when entertaining a small group of friends, or used as a game table when it's your turn to host the afternoon bridge club. The conversion can be made effortlessly and instantly. Just rotate the top, pull up, and rotate it again in the opposite direction to lock fixed position.

For its design alone, this chest would be an asset in a living room, dining room, or hall. But that's just half the story. It has a bonus feature, a dining table that is large enough for a dinner party, neatly concealed.

Each door splits in the middle and folds back to reveal storage for six leaves needed to extend the table to its full 104 inches. And, there is extra storage space inside.

ture to work for you. For the price of one piece of furniture, you actually get two pieces. For example, there is a china hutch which conceals an 87x38-inch table. This one piece of furniture provides roomy storage for china and crystal and comfortable dining space for nine.

If floor space is a real decorating problem in your home, let dual-purpose furniture solve it for you. If you love to entertain but find it nerve-wracking in cramped quarters, do it graciously with versatile furniture. Now on the market, you can purchase a flip-top table that doubles its size to make a roomy 78x40-inch dining table. But, when not needed for formal sit-down dinners, it can be pushed against a wall or placed behind a sofa to act as a table for two, a trim console, or a serving board for buffet suppers.

To further aid you in your entertaining endeavors, you might choose one of the beautifully designed storage chests. It will be perfectly at home in the living room and will be particularly convenient when guests drop by. With the top extended on both sides, the chest automatically becomes a buffet-server complete with a heat-resistant, stain-resistant top.

If your home or apartment is like most others today, storage may well be your most pressing problem. Dual-purpose furniture has more than one answer for storage problems—bookcase headboards that eliminate the necessity of having bedside tables, cocktail and end tables that serve as storage tables, and benches and ottomans that provide extra pull-up seating as well as additional storage space.

Almost every apartment or small home has some room that could benefit from the functional qualities of one of the many examples of dual-purpose furniture. These pieces are the perfect items with which to begin collecting furniture because you not only get two pieces for the price of one, but they are also so versatile that they may be used in almost any room of the house. They also come in compact, small-scaled sizes which add space-saving characteristics to their valuable mobility and double-duty qualities.

furniture that can fit into many arrangements

Budget decorating means getting the most value for your money. This does not mean buying three rooms of furniture for $399. Instead, it means purchasing good-quality furniture in a timeless style.

However, quality furniture is seldom low priced, and if it is to fit into your budget, you must collect it one piece at a time rather than a roomful at a time. To do this, keep your total decorating goal in mind, shop around to see what's available at the best price, and make up your mind to use your own time and energy in money-saving do-it-yourself projects.

The floor plans on the opposite page are good examples of how quality furniture can be collected as a lifetime investment. Thorough planning, wise shopping, and versatile furniture designs are essential keys needed to collect furniture as a lifetime investment. Notice that even though the living situation changes in each plan, every piece of furniture remains functional and essential to the plan.

The first plan is an 11x16 room, typical of any efficiency, one-, or two-bedroom apartment. However, the decorating strategy employed is not typical.

Our young married couple rented their first apartment and began furnishing it with a dedicated eye toward the future and a disciplined hand on the pocketbook.

The floor plan left a little to be desired. It did not have a foyer, so the newlyweds built a room divider for less than $15, using strips of 1x2-inch lumber, eyelet screws, and colorful textured yarn. Placed in front of the door, the room divider separated the living room from the entrance and provided additional privacy.

The major portion of the decorating budget was spent for a quality sleeper-sofa which transformed the living room into a bedroom for overnight guests. To complete the seating requirements, they purchased two leatherlike vinyl director's chairs for under $30 each. For informal dining for two or buffet suppers, they purchased an inexpensive laminated Parson's table and grouped it with two side chairs for dining and extra pull-up seating. To unite the conversation area, our young couple shopped for a 4x6-foot area rug. They found imitation sisal, Oriental, and fur; braided, shag, plush, and sculptured rugs, ranging in price from $15 to $50. However, authentic Oriental, Moroccan, Rya, or fur rugs the same size could be purchased for around $150 if your beginning budget would allow for such a smashing accent.

The remainder of their decorating "essentials" developed from do-it-yourself projects. A small, premature antique commode, found in a secondhand store, was refinished and used for additional storage space. For a cocktail table, our ingenious couple bought a metal office wastebasket, turned it upside down and covered it with part of a roll of $6 cork wallpaper, applied with rubber cement, and topped it with a 24-inch square piece of ½-inch thick Belgian plate glass, all of which cost less than $30. The remaining wallpaper was used to decorate one small wall of the foyer.

Within a short period of time, our couple, tired of apartment living, moved into a duplex. Because they had purchased versatile furniture in the beginning, they were able to use everything from the apartment and chose to add to their collection. They purchased a two-seater sofa to match the original sofa and an occasional table, and they built a bookcase unit from enameled lumber and ¼-inch glass shelving.

In a few years, this same couple bought a house and filled the extra space with a few more purchases—an occasional chair, a dining table, and another pair of their original dining chairs. At this time, they also chose to discard the $15 yarn room divider and purchase a walnut cylinder for the base of the cocktail table.

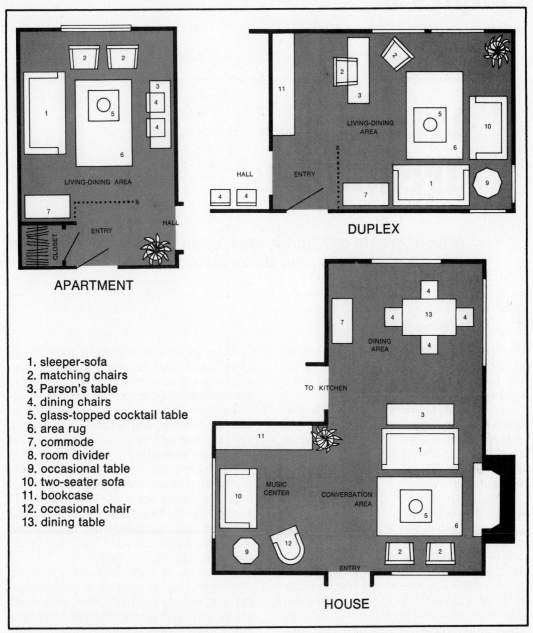

APARTMENT

DUPLEX

HOUSE

1. sleeper-sofa
2. matching chairs
3. Parson's table
4. dining chairs
5. glass-topped cocktail table
6. area rug
7. commode
8. room divider
9. occasional table
10. two-seater sofa
11. bookcase
12. occasional chair
13. dining table

When furniture is chosen for its good style, quality construction, and versatility, it becomes a lifetime investment. These floor plans illustrate how it is possible to "have your cake and eat it, too," even on a budget.

Keep your decorating goal foremost in mind. Know when you buy a chair that it will be used now in a conversation area in the living room and later in the den or bedroom. Purchase the essentials first—a sofa and chair. For additional versatility, buy multipurpose furniture; the Parson's table used in this instance had a different function in each plan—as a dining table or buffet server, a desk, and a console. Buy name brand merchandise. Here, it was possible to purchase both the matching two-seater sofa and the second pair of dining chairs years after the original items were purchased because quality lines carry open-stock merchandise.

chapter 5

Window Treatments

How to create attractive, inexpensive window treatments that add beauty to your decorating scheme.

Your choice of window treatments is limited only by your imagination and ingenuity, and the amount of money you have budgeted for the project.

Although the primary function of a window is to provide ventilation, natural light, and an outdoor view, the ideal window treatment also affords privacy, adds beauty to the room, and complements its furnishings and colors.

First, you must decide what you want to do with the window. Has your window a scenic view that you would like to frame as a painting, or does it have a no-view that you want to conceal? Do you have structural elements around the window or in the room that you would like to minimize, or windows of different shapes and sizes that you would prefer to standardize? You can overcome all these problems with the correct window treatment.

Most stores carry a good selection of draperies and curtains in many sizes. If you plan to buy ready-made rather than to make them yourself, you will save money if you can use these stock offerings. Any that are special-ordered and custom-made will cost more because of the labor involved in making them.

Then, determine how much you want to spend on a total decorating project. You will have a greater freedom of choice if you are embarking on a total decorating project, rather than having to conform to an existing scheme, but whatever the situation, the cost will be minimized if you shop wisely and patiently.

There are many types of window treatments to choose from (see next page), many of which are quite inexpensive. If you are nimble-fingered and can paint and sew, or if there is a handyman in the house who can install brackets and rods, your dollars will go still further.

The room at right features a window treatment that is elegant in appearance, yet simple to sew. If you wish, you could use an end-of-bolt sale fabric or one of the many other economy fabrics that are suitable: printed or striped bed sheets; striped mattress ticking or sailcloth; for a bathroom or a child's room, turkish towels or terry cloth by the yard. The tieback overdraperies are shirred on a wooden rod and trimmed with black cotton fringe. Unbleached muslin is stretched tight on rods at top and bottom. The only sewing involved with the overdraperies is hemming.

types of windows and window treatments

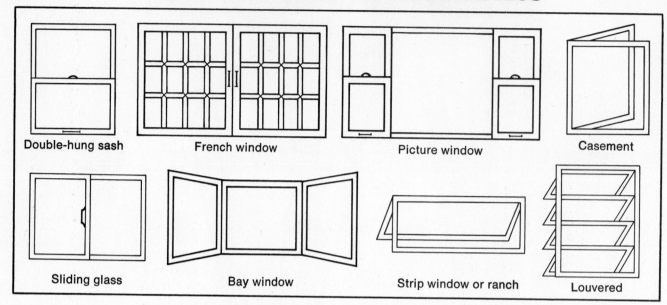

Double-hung sash

French window

Picture window

Casement

Sliding glass

Bay window

Strip window or ranch

Louvered

1. Hung from a traverse rod, draperies open from center toward outer edge of window. May be used alone, over shirred or traverse glass curtains, or with cafes. 2. Hung from a one-way draw traverse rod, drapery draws to one side of window. 3. Valance, pinch-pleated exactly like draw draperies, covers drapery heading and conceals drapery rods, hardware, and window trim. 4. Can be sill, apron, or floor length of any sheer fabric; shirred on rod and hung next to glass. 5. Under-draperies of sheer or medium-weight fabric, and overdraperies, usually of heavier fabric, both hung on traverse rods. 6. Short curtains or draperies, hung in pairs or multiple tiers, with pleated, scalloped, or tubular-pleated tops. Hung by rings on cafe rods in brass or bronze. 7. Cafe curtains cover lower part of window; overdraperies may hang straight or be held back with brass holdbacks or tiebacks. 8. Ruffled tie-back curtains are of sheer or medium-weight material, shirred on a single rod, with or without a valance.

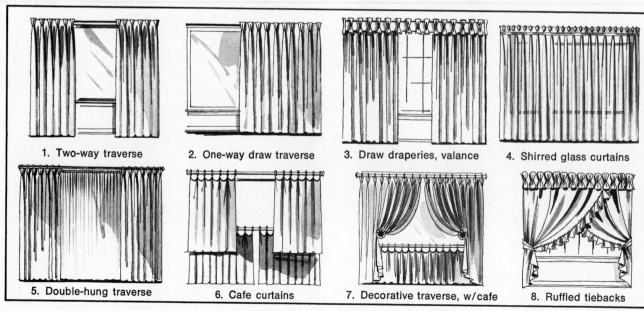

1. Two-way traverse

2. One-way draw traverse

3. Draw draperies, valance

4. Shirred glass curtains

5. Double-hung traverse

6. Cafe curtains

7. Decorative traverse, w/cafe

8. Ruffled tiebacks

The decorating dollar will go much further for the homemaker who can make her own draperies and curtains. Very often you can find good-quality fabrics, remnants, and discontinued patterns at marked-down prices. Whether lined or unlined, these fabrics can be expertly tailored by anyone.

Although lining adds to the initial cost, it is a wise investment in the long run. Lining protects drapery fabric from soiling and sun fading, adds body to any fabric, ensures complete privacy, and gives all windows a more uniform appearance from the outside.

HOW TO MEASURE FOR DRAPERIES AND CURTAINS

When you've decided what type of treatment you want, and have determined the area it will cover, install the rods and hardware. Then measure.

Next, take the length measurement and add seven inches to this figure for hemming and heading in draperies (ten inches for double hems if you are measuring for curtains). Also include extra yardage to ensure matching patterns if the fabric has a repeat pattern and for straightening the ends after each cut.

Now determine the width measurement. Measure the rod including the return—the section that curves around the corner to the wall. To ensure adequate fullness, double this figure. However, if you are installing unlined draperies or curtains of lightweight fabric, you should multiply the width to two-and-a-half or three.

The figure you now have is the total number of inches needed to adequately cover the window. To obtain the number of panels needed, divide this figure by the width of the fabric you plan to use. For example, if the window is 99 inches wide, the fabric will have to be 198 inches wide. And, since the fabric you plan to use comes in 36-inch widths, you will have to sew several panels together. Divide 198 by 35 (fabric width minus two ½-inch seam allow-

ances per panel). You now know that you'll need six 36-inch panels. To determine the amount of fabric needed, multiply the number of panels by the length measurement and divide this figure by 36 to convert it to yards.

AND NOW THE CONSTRUCTION

Once you've purchased the fabric, lay it on a flat surface for cutting. Cut the first panel carefully and use it as a guide for the rest. Lay the first panel on top of the fabric and carefully match patterns. Remember to cut away the selvage edge or clip it so that the seams won't pucker and the draperies will hang straight.

If you are lining the draperies, cut the lining fabric three and a half inches shorter and six inches narrower than the overall dimensions of the drapery panel.

To make unlined draperies and curtains, turn under ½ inch at the side edges and press. Next, turn back a 1½-inch hem, baste, and hem either by hand or machine. Now, hem the bottom by turning under 3 inches; then turning under another 3 inches, and stitching a double hem. To finish the top the easy way, purchase commercial pleater tape heading and stitch the right side of the tape to the right side of the fabric. Turn the tape to the inside, press, and stitch along the sides and edge of the tape under the hook pockets. Or, make a casing and heading for the rod to slide through. Turn the top under ½ inch and turn under again 2½ inches. Hem by hand or machine. Next, on the machine, stitch a line ½ inch from the top edge.

Lined draperies are made very much the same as are unlined draperies. Hem the bottoms of the drapery panel and the lining separately. Next, pin the right side of the lining to the right side of the drapery fabric and sew down each side, with the top edges even. Center the lining so 1¼-inch hems turn back on either side of the panel. Attach the pleater tape heading as before, and the project is completed.

shutters

Shutters combine function and style and offer endless decorating possibilities. The initial cost may seem high, but the life of a shutter makes it a good long-term investment. They can be used instead of glass curtains, or in combination with draperies, shades, or valances. They add character and architectural interest, can disguise problem windows, and conceal radiators or air conditioners. They allow complete flexibility in light control and ventilation and, at the same time, ensure privacy.

Shutters come in a variety of finishes—painted, natural wood, or unfinished—and are available in a wide range of stock sizes, or they can be special-ordered in custom sizes. The individual panels may have movable or fixed louvers—cane, mesh,

Shutters stained in a dark wood tone cover the window in photo below. Fabric-covered panels at each side are hinged together in pairs. Fabric is stapled to frames of stock dimensional lumber.

solid panel, stained glass, or fabric inserts.

More than one type of shutter may be used in a single window treatment. If you have a window with no view or an ugly view, use a combination of shutters with fabric inserts to cover the window, and solid panel shutters below that extend to the floor. The panels with fabric inserts will conceal the view but allow light to filter through, and the solid panel shutters can hide shelves for storage. Or, you could use shutters with adjustable louvers and ones with metal mesh or cane inserts below to conceal the radiator or air conditioner without interrupting air flow. Proper air flow is important especially in small areas.

Shutters are expensive if custom installed but are relatively inexpensive if you finish and install them yourself. First, measure the window carefully. In order to have shutters fit inside the edges of the window casing, you will probably have to do some trimming. This type of installation is more popular than having the shutters hang over the window opening. Usually,

you can trim as much as one-half inch from each side of a shutter panel and two inches from top and bottom. Measure the window carefully and trim enough so that they fit exactly inside window casing.

After fitting but prior to hanging the shutters, apply the finish. If you choose to use paint, apply a wash coat of shellac before painting. Your paint will go further and the job will have a more professional look. Removable-panel shutters may be finished easily with either spray or brush-on finishes. However, louvered shutters are more easily done with spray finishes. If you use a stain finish, always use a protective topcoat of clear lacquer spray.

If you are using removable-panel shutters, consider fabric panel inserts. They add color and pattern and are simple to sew. Cut the fabric about twice as wide as the opening in the shutter. Make a narrow hem at the top and the bottom, just wide enough to slide the rods through. Then, slip the ends of the rod into the holes already in the shutter frame.

easy shutter installation

Mortise in hinges by using hinge as template. Draw around it, score along line with chisel. Cut mortise to depth of closed hinge.

Set shutter panels in place on shim, such as blade from combination square, and mark hinge locations on casing with a knife.

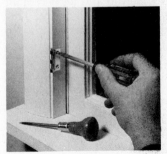

Pull out pin of loose pin hinge and mount hinge leaf at mark. Use sharp awl to make starter holes for screws; center holes.

When hung, center panels will probably overlap slightly. Mark overlap, remove and plane away half of excess from each panel.

shades

Shades can be an inexpensive decorating tool if you use decorative ones that provide the complete window treatment. If your budget allows, you can use them in combination with draperies, glass curtains, cafe curtains, or shutters.

There are styles to suit any decorating mood—traditional, provincial, or contemporary. In all of these styles, you will find shade materials that are plain or textured; opaque or translucent; and in striped, patterned, or solid colors, which range all the way from the most subdued neutrals to dramatic decorator colors. Each of these can be neatly tailored, or trimmed with braid or fringe, or can have shaped hems, scalloped borders, and cornices to add an even greater look of professional decorating.

TYPES OF SHADES

Although window shades come in a limitless range of variations, there are only four basic types from which to choose: the pulldown shade, the Austrian shade, the Roman shade, and the bottoms-up shade. 1. Pulldown shades are the most familiar type of window shade and offer the greatest opportunity to imaginatively decorate your windows with a minimum amount of time and expense.

2 & 3. Austrian and Roman shades are not attached to shade rollers as are other types of shades; instead, they are regulated with a cord, rings, and pulleys. The Austrian shade is shirred and draped when lowered or raised; it adds a dramatic accent to a formal room with traditional furnishings. The Roman shade falls into deep pleats when it is raised. This type of window shade is compatible with country or contemporary furnishings. Either shade type may be used alone or in combination with matching draperies.

4. Bottoms-up shades are mounted from the bottom of the window and are regulated by tracks at either side. This mounting offers greater flexibility in light control,

ventilation, and privacy. Depending on the material that is used, they are similar in cost to pulldown shades and are also well suited to a large number of contemporary rooms.

HOW TO MEASURE FOR SHADES

Shade measurements must be accurate in order to get a proper fit and operate easily. Measure the exact distance between the points where brackets are to be placed. For an outside hang, place brackets so there is a 1½- to 2-inch overlap on each side of the casement. Shade length should be the full length of the window opening plus 12 inches to permit the shade to be drawn full length without any danger of it being torn from the roller. Be sure to measure each window; even though they appear identical, there may be a variation in size.

HOW TO CARE FOR SHADES

Shades require little care and upkeep. Most of those available today are washable.

When the time comes that your shades need a thorough cleaning, it is a simple operation. Remove the shade, place it on a flat surface, and wash a small area at a time. Wipe each cleaned section with a damp sponge before starting on the next one. When one entire side is completed, turn the shade over and repeat the process on the opposite side. When the cleaning is finished, hang the shade and pull it down full length and let it remain this way overnight, or until thoroughly dry. Then roll it up all the way to the top and let it remain in this position for about 12 hours. This cleaning procedure will restore shades to their original appearance.

HOW TO DECORATE SHADES

Decorative shades definitely add a special touch to almost any window. But, if you buy them ready-made in a shade shop or department store, they are oftentimes prohibitively expensive. You can create the same effect at a much lower cost if you use your own "cut and paste" creative talents, an inexpensive vinyl window shade, and a few yards of fringe, ribbon, or lightweight fabric.

For the ultimate in the one-fabric look, use window shades with the fabric of your choice laminated onto the shade material. For this application, tightly woven fabrics such as cotton, rayon, or linen are best. If too heavy a fabric is used, the shade will be too bulky when raised. But, if the fabric is too sheer or porous, the glue might show through the fabric. This is a decorating job that is best done by a professional, but there are products on the market aimed at the do-it-yourselfer who wants to be economical by doing her own laminating. For a truly coordinated look, use fabrics that match the draperies, cafe curtains, valances, bedspreads, or upholstery fabrics in the room.

There are pulldown shades of vinyl-coated fiber glass yarns specially woven into a window-screen-type pattern that permit you to see out, but block the view into the room. These shades reduce solar heat penetration, fading, and glare, which will aid your budgeting by reducing heating and cooling costs. If you want to add a decorative touch to these otherwise tailored white shades, you can use press-on braid or fringe, appliquéd designs, or stenciled motifs that harmonize with the total window treatment. Stenciled designs on shades or valances add a personal touch in almost any room. This is a project that can be accomplished in a professional manner, even by those who claim to have no artistic flare. If you stick to only one col-

Fashion flowers, stems, and leaves from embroidery floss. Stitch or glue them to the shade. Tack row of floss above the hem.

Weave wide satin or velvet ribbons through wood-slat blinds to create a pleasing design. Then, staple ribbons at top and bottom.

or, it will be simpler because each additional color requires a stencil. Let fabrics or patterns elsewhere in the room guide you in the selection of a design or motif. Trace the design carefully and accurately. Transfer the traced design to heavy cardboard. Using a mat knife, carefully cut out the stencil design. Position the stencil on the shade and secure it with masking tape. Use textile paint, and apply it with a stencil brush held in an upright position. With a circular motion, work the paint into the stencil motif. If you are using more than one color, be sure that the first one is completely dry before applying the next. After the stenciling has dried for 24 hours, iron it at a low temperature to set the color. With a pressing cloth placed over the design, iron over each part of the design for six minutes.

Appliquéd designs can transform the least expensive shades into an exciting and important part of your room's decor. Use the most important element in the pattern of a vinyl-coated wallpaper or a tightly woven printed fabric. Before cutting a fabric design, spray the wrong side of the fabric with an acrylic spray, or, on the wrong side, outline the design with colorless nail polish. This will prevent the edges from raveling. Use small sharp scissors and cut out the design carefully. Arrange and rearrange them on the shade until you have the most pleasing effect. Then, apply glue to the entire back side of each cutout. Be sure that they are completely covered with glue before you press them firmly in place on the shade. Smooth each motif carefully to make sure there are no air bubbles between the shade and appliqué. After the pasting has been completed and the glue has dried, spray an extra coating of the acrylic spray over each design. You may like to add one or more rows of press-on adhesive braid or fringe in matching or contrasting colors for a border effect.

This one-pattern look was achieved by using the same fabric on both the laminated shade and the upholstered chair. Sheer overdraperies emphasize colors without detracting from the pattern.

cornices and valances

There are many ways in which cornices and valances can aid your window treatments. They give a finished look to a window treatment, improve window dimensions, and conceal brackets, rods, and rollers.

A cornice is a shallow, boxlike structure, usually made of wood. It can be painted, stained, covered, or padded. The border design may be straight, curved, or scalloped. A single cornice may be window or ceiling height and may extend across one or more windows. The cornice style you choose depends on the room, its furnishings, and your budget.

A valance is a strip of fabric that hangs above a window. It may be straight or scalloped, draped, pleated, or shirred. Depending on the design and fabric, a valance may be informal or formal.

Cornices and valances are the "extra" ingredient in your window treatment. They add much to the appearance of your room, but they also add extra expenses to your treatment because they are usually combined with some other treatment. However there are ways to create the expensive decorator look on a limited budget.

Moldings or sculptured motifs can be purchased in department stores and lumberyards and applied to cornices before painting to give a hand-carved effect. Or, if you want a padded cornice, build it from the least expensive grade of lumber. For a padding, tack or staple a layer of foam rubber or cotton batting to the outside and cover it with sale fabric.

Make your own valances from firm inexpensive materials such as felt, leatherlike vinyl, vinyl-coated fabrics, shade cloth, or canvas. Make a casing at the top and thread it on a curtain rod. Cut the border design of your choice and trim with fringe, braid, or appliquéd designs.

To reduce glare of a window wall, use a plywood cornice with filigree panels hung on a double ceiling track so they can slide open.

A cornice covered with felt and edged with ball fringe hangs over a window shade that is trimmed with vinyl-coated wallpaper.

chapter 6

Floors &
Floor Coverings

How to transform an expensive floor covering idea into an inexpensive but equally effective budget treatment.

Floors anchor and unite a room's furnishings and are therefore vitally important to the success of your decorating scheme. But, if you are living in a house or apartment that has been previously occupied, you are undoubtedly living in an atmosphere of wall-to-wall mystery. For instance, that spreading stain in the middle of the living room carpeting that makes you wonder if the ultramarine blue carpeting wasn't installed over a sunken oil tanker. Or, those long scratches on the hardwood floors that give you reason to suspect the previous tenants of hosting Roller Derby parties every Saturday afternoon. Regardless of how much you may dislike your present floor, you may feel compelled to make do with what you have because you feel that any change would surely represent a large expenditure of your time, energy, and money. This is not necessarily true. Giving your floor a new look need not be expensive. Just study the examples in this chapter, shop wisely, be willing to use a little elbow grease, and you can have a floor that is both exciting and inexpensive.

The illustration at right shows how this can be done. For example, you can duplicate the black and white tile floor with either vinyl-asbestos tile for a nominal amount or asphalt tile if you feel you must be extremely budget conscious.

You can save on the two room-size rugs if you shop the floor covering stores for remnants. One good shopper, for example, paid $70 for a 10x11-foot piece of carpeting similar to the one in the illustration, and paid only $10 to have it bound. She saved around $150.

The expensive rya accent rug might pose a more complicated problem; but you can duplicate it if you are prepared to do the work. You can buy a kit for under $85 and make the rug yourself. Or, you can save even more by purchasing the materials separately for less than $50. (If you use the latter method, buy a rya pillow kit for under $9 and first master the skill.)

The hardwood floors were emphasized rather than hidden. This isn't difficult and you'll be amazed at how attractive the most deplorable floors can look once the old finish is removed and wax is applied.

So, no matter which type of floor you decide upon, soft, resilient, or rigid, remember that wise shopping and do-it-yourself creativity will save you as much as 70 per cent of the retail cost.

carpeting

Never before has there been such a large selection of carpet colors, patterns, fibers, or prices. Yet, instead of making it easier to shop for floor coverings, the huge selection and strange vocabulary can confuse an uninformed shopper. After one session in the carpet shop looking over hundreds of style samples made of fibers with unfamiliar names, such as acrylic, modacrylic, polypropylene, polyester, and saran, each wielding promises of "miracles" and conflicting claims, you may decide it takes a chemist to select the proper carpeting!

This is not true. If you deal with a reliable store and salesman, there are only four decisions to make. Two of them concern appearance—selecting the style you like best and the color and texture best suited to your home. The other two concern value—getting the best quality at a price you can best afford. The logical place to start is to sit down and figure out just what you want in the way of floor coverings for your home.

There are only three types of soft surface floor coverings: wall-to-wall carpeting, room-size rugs, and area rugs.

1. Wall-to-wall carpeting covers the entire floor surface and makes the room appear larger because of the unbroken area of color. This type of floor covering helps unify a room and minimize many of the architectural eyesores.

2. Room-size rugs are sold in standard sizes from 6x9 to 12x18 feet, or you can have one cut from any roll of carpeting. With this type of floor covering, you will have a border of floor showing around the edges of the rug—about 8 inches in a small room and 10 to 12 inches in a large one. A room-size rug offers you the extra advantage of turning the rug around from time to time to evenly distribute the traffic wear.

3. Area rugs range from strictly utilitarian to designers' works of art. They come in a wide variety of colors, patterns, shapes, and sizes. The size of an area rug usually ranges from 3x5 to 12x15 feet, but the size you choose depends on the size of the area and the size of the furniture grouping the rug will define.

CONSIDER APPEARANCE FIRST

First, think of how your floor covering will look in the room. Unless you like its looks, performance and price won't seem very important. Select a color family that you really like. Look at all the possibilities in this color choice. Then, narrow your selection to three or four shades and take the samples home to study them in relation to your furnishings and lighting.

When shopping for carpeting, don't be confused by the wide variety. Remember the key: "the deeper, the denser, the better."

Also consider the practical side of color selection. If you have several children who track dirt into the house regularly, select a color that won't show soil easily—a medium color rather than one that is very dark or very light. Or choose color mixtures, tweeds, and multicolor patterns in tight, dense textures, such as twists, loops, or sculptured designed surfaces. This is true, also, for carpeting in heavily trafficked areas, such as living rooms, family rooms, and halls.

DETERMINE THE AMOUNT OF WEAR

Next, consider the amount of wear you'll give your carpeting and how long you'll want the carpet to last. This should determine what fiber you choose as well as what weight, quality, and price of carpeting you select. In rooms that receive very light use, you can get good service from economy carpeting, priced in the low-end-per-square-yard price range. Carpeting whose price falls in the medium-price range is generally suitable for all areas of a home that receive an average amount of wear, such as bedrooms, dining rooms, and some little-used living rooms. But for those areas that get hard use—living rooms, halls, and stairs—top-quality carpeting is essential for long wear.

Some manufacturers now produce three price grades of carpeting with identical texture and color so that you can have the same color and texture of carpeting in every room of the house but don't have to pay top-dollar prices for all of it. This means a lower overall cost for you.

If you are considering wall-to-wall carpeting, always select it from the middle range on up to get full value from the installation. And remember, a good room-size rug, which can be turned to equalize wear, is a better buy than cheap wall-to-wall carpeting that won't last.

Quality is certainly a determining factor in the life of any carpeting, but don't forget the carpet padding. It adds comfort, quiet, and insulation as well as acting as a "shock absorber" to prolong the life of the carpeting.

There are two types of padding available: the felted type made of hair or jute and the one made of rubber. A 40-ounce felt pad or a one-quarter to three-eighths inch rubber pad is suitable for most homes. The cost of padding is often quoted in the cost of the installed carpeting, but if it isn't, plan to spend at least another $1.25 a square yard for padding.

HOW TO RECOGNIZE QUALITY

The best single clue to quality is the basic rule, "the deeper, the denser, the better." This refers to the surface pile—the part you see and walk on. Dense pile, with the tufts closely packed together, wears longest because the yarns support each other, resist bending and abrasion.

Use your hands and eyes to test a sample. Bend the sample back to see the closeness of the construction. The less backing visible, the denser the pile.

The construction of your carpet is also important. Carpets are usually constructed in one of three ways: woven, tufted, or knitted. One type is not necessarily any better than the others, provided each is constructed well. All three types will have a backing. The backing holds the carpet together and prevents stretching, shrinking, and buckling. Most good-quality tufted carpets will have an extra laminated layer of backing for greater strength.

The type of fiber used does not, by itself, guarantee the quality of the carpet. However, various fibers have their own characteristics that do affect the carpet's performance and life span.

Wool is the "classic" carpet fiber—the yardstick used for measuring other fibers. It offers a balance of desirable characteristics: resiliency, abrasion resistance, warmth, and soil resistance.

The synthetic fibers are the acrylics and modacrylics, nylon, polypropylene, olefin, and rayon.

1. Acrylics and modacrylics closely resemble wool in their warmth and feel. These synthetics are noted for their high soil and stain resistance. They're resilient, quick-drying, and long-wearing. They resist crushing and clean well.

2. Polyester is another synthetic fiber that resembles wool and acrylic. It is exceptionally long-wearing, easy to maintain, soil resistant, and takes color well to give you clear, bright colors.

3. Nylon is noted for its good wearing qualities and ease of care. It is the most durable of all carpet fibers and takes color well. It also resists staining and pilling.

4. Polypropylene olefin is a very strong, lightweight carpet fiber that features good abrasion resistance and stain resistance. It resembles nylon and is most often used in outdoor and kitchen carpeting.

Carpeting can also be made from fiber blends. In blending natural and synthetic fibers, you are able to get the best qualities of each fiber used. For example, nylon may be blended with wool for reinforcement in a "70/30" ratio. The finished carpet will look and feel most like its predominant fiber, wool, but it will also be more durable, resistant to soil, and easier to care for than would a pure wool carpet.

Generally, at least 20 percent of a fiber must be used before its characteristics are apparent. But, to be sure of its content, always read the tag on the back of the carpeting. This tag gives you the brand, pattern, and color names, the fiber content, where it was manufactured, and whether or not the carpeting has been permanently mothproofed. Save these tags for reference when cleaning or repairing.

HOW TO CARE FOR YOUR CARPETING

The amount of care needed to keep carpeting and rugs in good condition depends on the color and style you select (a white, plush carpeting will require more care than a brown tweed carpeting), the location of your home (the dirtier the air in your area, the more you will have to vacuum), and the amount of traffic in your room (naturally, the more traffic, the more dirt will be tracked in, and the more you will have to vacuum). Depending upon the variables—color, texture, traffic, and location—you may need to vacuum lightly only two times a week or as often as every day. But, all carpeting re-

quires heavy-duty vacuuming—seven slow, strokes over each area—once a week to remove soil that cuts fibers.

Your vacuum cleaner removes some, but not all, of the dirt from your carpeting. Eventually, it will require professional cleaning. If you have wall-to-wall carpeting, the service will come to your home for on-the-spot cleaning, or if you have room-size rugs or area rugs, a professional service can thoroughly clean them at the plant. But professional cleaning should be considered every 12 to 18 months.

Between professional cleanings, you may wish to clean the carpeting yourself. You may use the dry method, sprinkling a special powder-type carpet cleaner on the floor and then vacuuming. Or, use the wet method, sprinkling the carpet with two heaping tablespoons of a light, natural detergent mixed with one gallon of water. Apply this solution sparingly and gently sponge it onto the fibers. Do not allow the backing of the carpeting to become wet. Dry the carpeting as quickly as possible, using forced air from your vacuum cleaner. Avoid frequent use of the wet method as the detergent produces a residue that causes the carpeting to resoil. This residue cannot be rinsed off.

SPECIAL CARPET PROBLEMS

Despite the care and attention you give carpeting, certain minor problems are inevitable. However, most are correctable.

For soiled or stained carpeting the best advice is to call in a professional cleaning service, but if you want to try it yourself, follow the stain removal chart on page 61 and then clean the carpeting thoroughly. Some worn spots can be camouflaged by rearranging the furniture or by covering them with an area rug. Crushed or matted spots caused by furniture can be corrected by holding a steam iron about a half inch above the spot for about one minute.

Other problems, such as shedding and pilling, are common to new carpeting. These problems will end within a few weeks after regular and thorough vacuuming. But remember, never pull a tuft that extends above the surface—clip it.

resilient floors

Resilient floor covering is the second major type of floor covering. No longer restricted to bathroom and kitchen use, wood-grain, random-width wood, parquet, marble, brick, cobblestone, and terrazzo patterns, in decorator colors, offer unlimited decorating possibilities to every room in your house.

Resilient floor coverings include inlaid linoleum, vinyl, rubber, vinyl asbestos, asphalt, and cork. All of these products come in two basic forms: 9- or 12-inch tiles and 6-, 9-, and 12-foot wide sheets. Tiles are a natural for do-it-yourself installation, especially paper-covered adhesive back tiles. They adhere without additional mastic to any floor that is in good condition and cost only about 19 cents a tile or $36.48 for a 9x12 room. The lack of seams is a real plus in favor of the sheet floorings. There are no places for dirt to catch and collect, so maintenance is simplified. A few of these may be scissor-cut for self-installation.

There are endless decorating possibilities open to you when you choose one of the many types of resilient floors, each of which comes in a variety of colors, textures, patterns, and prices.

When selecting a resilient floor covering, you must consider more than color and pattern and whether or not you want it in tile or sheet form. You must also consider durability, cost, ease of maintenance, and installation. To choose the floor covering that best fits your needs and budget, learn the characteristics of each resilient flooring material—vinyl, asbestos tile, asphalt tile, homogeneous vinyl tile, linoleum, sheet vinyl, or poured vinyl.

TYPES OF RESILIENT FLOORS

1. Vinyl asbestos tile is the most widely used flooring because of its durability and resistance to grease, alkali, and staining. Also, it requires a minimum of maintenance, and it is comparatively inexpensive. This is a favorite with do-it-yourselfers because of its easy installation.

2. An asphalt tile floor's most remarkable feature is its low cost. While its wear resistance is rated excellent, soil resistance and cleanability are rated poor to fair. It's not recommended for kitchens because of its lack of resiliency.

3. Homogeneous vinyl tile, sometimes called solid or pure vinyl tile, is more expensive than either of the two above. It is the most flexible of all resilient tiles, and it is exceptionally durable. It is easy to clean and maintain, and is rated excellent for wear and soil resistance.

4. Linoleum flooring, a time-proven flooring material, still remains a favorite with many homeowners. It will give years of service because of its ease of maintenance and its resistance to wear, soil, and grease. It is not resistant to alkalis.

5. If you like continuous surface flooring with no seams to collect dirt and dust, be sure to consider sheet vinyl. Although it is more expensive than vinyl asbestos, it is very durable, resistant to wear, soil, grease, and alkalis, and it is easy to maintain. It is quiet and comfortable underfoot, and comes in many patterns and colors.

6. If you want a perfectly seamless floor, there is a vinyl available that is poured directly onto the subfloor. This liquid material is applied to the floor in several different coats. You can create your own individual pattern by scattering plastic chips on the surface before the last coat is applied. This is no more difficult to do than painting a floor, but you must work out a good schedule so the successive steps are carried out on time. This type of flooring is easy to maintain.

HOW TO CARE FOR RESILIENT FLOORS

Resilient floors are built to take a lot of traffic with minimum maintenance, but a little regular care will keep them looking bright and attractive.

Sweep daily with a soft brush, broom, or vacuum to remove dirt that might scratch the surface. Wipe up spills as they occur, using a paper towel dipped in clear water. Damp mop with clear water to remove fine surface soil. If stubborn spots continue to be a problem, consult the stain removal chart on the opposite page for first aid treatment.

Every four to six weeks give your floor a thorough cleaning, using a mild detergent or one of the regular floor cleaners if you want to clean and wax at the same time. Always rinse the floor after washing with a detergent or mild soap.

All resilient floors need regular waxing. On all resilient materials, except cork and vinyl-cork tile, use a good grade of water-emulsion wax, applied in thin coats. For cork tile, use a solvent-based wax especially made for cork.

When applying wax, keep in mind that a thin application will wear better, dry harder, and scuff less than a thick coat. It is also less work for you.

If your resilient floor is old, it may be cloudy or discolored because it was cleaned too often with harsh cleaning compounds. You may clear up this condition by using a solution of white vinegar in water or a commercial floor cleaner and then waxing. Or, it may have layers of built-up wax and embedded dirt clouding the surface. If this is the case, rent an electric floor scrubber and use a good wax remover to speed up the job. Then, rinse thoroughly, let dry, and apply one or two thin coats of wax.

stain removal chart

61

CARPETING	
TYPE OF STAIN	**PROCEDURE**
Ball-point pen ink, butter, grease, oil, furniture polish.	Remove excess material, absorbing liquids, and scraping semisolids; sparingly apply solution of one teaspoon of neutral detergent or one teaspoon of white vinegar mixed with one quart of warm water. Dry carpet. Apply dry-cleaning solvent; dry again and brush gently.
Coffee, tea, milk, blood, egg, vomit, ice cream, sauces, salad dressing, chocolate.	Remove excess materials with blunt knife, apply a dry-cleaning fluid; dry carpet surface and, if necessary, repeat application of solvent. Dry carpet thoroughly with forced air from the vacuum cleaner and brush pile gently to restore its original texture.
Candy, soft drinks, alcoholic beverages, fruit stains, washable ink, urine, excrement.	Blot up liquids or scrape off semisolids. Apply either the vinegar-water solution or the detergent-water solution. Dry carpet and reapply solution, if necessary. Dry carpet and brush pile gently.
Tar, heavy grease, crayon, lipstick, paste shoe polish.	Remove excess material. Apply a dry-cleaning fluid; apply detergent-water solution or vinegar-water solution. Reapply dry-cleaning fluid. Dry carpet thoroughly and brush pile gently.
Varnish, shellac, paint.	For varnish and paint, blot excess with clean paper towel; apply few drops of turpentine to clean, dry cloth and dab lightly, working from the outer edge of the stain to the center. Apply nonflammable household dry-cleaning fluid. Let dry. For shellac, use denatured alcohol. Follow the same procedure.
Chewing gum.	Hold ice cube to gum until it becomes cold. Remove material with blunt knife and sponge lightly with nonflammable dry-cleaning fluid.
RESILIENT FLOORING	
TYPE OF STAIN	**PROCEDURE**
Mercurochrome, acids, alcoholic beverages, fruit stains, coffee.	Wash area with cloth dipped in floor cleaner and water, then rinse. If necessary, rub with 00 or 000 steel wool dipped in floor cleaner, rinse.
Rubber heel marks, shoe polish.	Rub lightly with 00 or 000 steel wool dipped in floor cleaner, then rinse. If this fails, dust with mild household abrasive cleaner, then rub with steel wool dipped in floor cleaner. Rinse. Polish when dry.
Dry-cleaning fluids, lacquer, nail polish remover, solvents, paint, varnish.	If freshly spilled, blot up immediately. Wash with cloth; dipped in floor cleaner, then rinse. If dry, remove excess with putty knife. Rub with 00 or 000 steel wool dipped in floor cleaner, then rinse. If this fails, dust with mild household abrasive cleaner, then rub with steel wool dipped in liquid cleaner. Rinse and polish when dry.
Asphalt, candle wax, candy, chewing gum, grease, oil, tar.	If dry, scrape with putty knife. Rub with fine steel wool dipped in floor cleaner, then rinse. If this fails, dust with mild household abrasive cleanser, then rub with fine steel wool dipped in liquid floor cleaner. Rinse and polish when dry. To make scraping gum easier freeze gum with ice; then scrape. Rub with steel wool and floor cleaner.
Cigarette burns, rust, mildew, blood, dye, grass.	Rub with 00 or 000 steel wool dipped in floor cleaner, then rinse. If this fails, dust with mild household abrasive cleanser, then rub with 00 or 000 steel wool in liquid cleaner. Rinse and polish when dry. If rust stain does not respond, use a 10 percent solution of oxalic acid. Then clean with floor cleaner and rinse.
Shellac	Wash with cloth dipped in floor cleaner, then rinse. If necessary, rub lightly with cloth dipped in alcohol, then rinse and polish when dry.
Urine	Use floor cleaner. If stain is old and does not respond, use 10 percent oxalic acid followed with floor cleaner.

rigid floors

RIGID FLOORS

The second group of hard-surface flooring is called rigid flooring. This group includes both hard and soft wood, marble, stone, brick, terrazzo, and mosaic tile.

Because they are so rarely seen, floors made of these materials are the "instant" personality makers of the floor covering field. If you've ever walked into someone's home for the first time and been surprised by a polished brick floor in the foyer or a mellow random-plank floor in a colonial family room, you'll remember the immediate impression of individuality.

As all rigid floors are installed permanently, you won't want to invest in them unless you own or are building your own home. But, if you are fortunate enough to have these floors already, emphasize them. They will do much in creating the individuality of your room's decor.

Well-polished wood floors help create a room's personality. Dark stain will enhance both the wood grain and colors in the room.

COMPARE THE COST

If you are living in your own home or are building a new home, consider rigid flooring. It is permanent, is easily maintained, adds immediate interest, and costs no more than soft or resilient floor coverings.

If you decide that the natural beauty of wood floors is your preference, you have many materials from which to choose. There are plain wood, strip floorings that are available in oak, beech, and maple. These are less expensive than the random-width plank oak floors that vary in price according to quality. Many people prefer the least expensive of the plank floorings because the surface imperfections more nearly duplicate an Early American atmosphere. Or, you may want select oak, walnut, teak, or maple solid parquet flooring in crosshatched, basket-weave, herringbone, or straight strip patterns. Less expensive, but equally attractive, are the prefinished parquet squares of 3-ply hardwood faced with oak, walnut, or cherry.

All four of these wood floors are comparable in price to what it would cost to have vinyl asbestos tiles professionally installed or what it would cost to install solid vinyl tile yourself. And, compared to the cost of wall-to-wall carpeting, most types of wood floorings do not cost more than medium-priced carpeting.

HOW TO RECONDITION WOOD FLOORS

You can give almost any wood floor a new lease on life as long as the floorboards themselves are in sound condition. And, reconditioning wood floors is both practical and economical.

To really cut costs, do it yourself. First, sand off the old finish and smooth up the wood with a rented sander. But, by all means, first try the floor sander in a closet or in some similar area, just in case you have a little trouble getting the hang of it. Before applying the finish, clean the floor thoroughly with the vacuum using a brush attachment. Then stain the floor to a dark color, using a brush or rag. Wipe off the remaining stain after five minutes. Then allow the stain to dry for twelve hours before applying a coat of varnish or wax or both.

However, if the old stain is in good condition, you may need to use only mineral spirits or naphtha and steel wool to remove the dirt and old wax. Wipe off the residue before it sets and then re-wax.

If you are really intent on refinishing the floors yourself, tell the sanding-equipment dealer the number of square feet you plan to refinish and the general condition of the floor. He can then advise you on the exact materials you will need.

If you own your home or if you have the landlord's permission, you can easily paint your wood floors if they have no particular beauty worth preserving. This is an easy and very inexpensive floor treatment for scarred floors, and it's an authentic treatment for an Early American decor. Thoroughly clean the floor with mineral spirits or naphtha and steel wool to remove all the old dirt and wax. With a brush, paint a strip around the baseboards, then do the rest of the floor with a roller. Apply at least two thin coats of a quality deck enamel and then wax the floor thoroughly.

After you have painted your floor with a tough enamel, you may want to embellish it further with either spatterwork or stencil designs. If so, this should be done before the floor is waxed.

Spatterwork, dating back to the colonial days of Cape Cod, is easy and fun to do. Paint the floor with enamel. When it is dry, give half the floor a second coat. When this section is nearly dry and still sticky, start spattering. Dip a very coarse paintbrush or long-handled whisk broom into the paint. Strike the brush sharply against a broomstick, holding it about twelve inches from the floor. Smaller spatters can be made by using less paint on the brush or holding the brush farther from the floor. After this side has dried, repeat the process on the other side. You may use one or more colors, depending on how many times you want to repeat the process. However, be sure that one coat of spatters is dry before applying the next. After the floor is finished and completely dry, wax it to a hard, brilliant shine.

Stencils are also possible but they require a steady hand, a good deal of patience, and a lot of practice. Buy stencil designs at any art supply store or draw your own on heavy cardboard and cut them out with a razor. Hold the stencil firmly in place with double-faced mastic tape. First practice on paper to make sure that the paint is neither too thin nor too thick. When you have mastered the technique of stencilling, try it on a clean floor. After the paint is thoroughly dry, wax the entire floor.

OTHER TYPES OF
RIGID FLOORING

Mosaic or ceramic tile is another common type of rigid flooring. With its many new patterns and colors, it is used throughout the house. In addition to its decorative qualities, ceramic tile is easily maintained and will last a lifetime. The cost of ceramic tile depends on the type of tile used and on the installation charges.

Waxed brick, stone, and slate floors can be extremely attractive in country kitchens, halls, foyers, living rooms, and dining rooms. Although they aren't the most comfortable underfoot, they are long wearing, easily maintained, and comparatively inexpensive, especially in the southwest regions of the United States.

Of all the types of rigid flooring, marble is the most expensive. Terrazzo, which is poured concrete made with chips of marble, is less expensive and can be used in halls, foyers, bathrooms, and other areas that receive a great deal of wear.

Remember that rigid flooring is a permanent investment. So, make certain that its color and pattern is one you'll want to live with forever. Compare its appearance, durability, maintenance, and cost with the other types of flooring and choose the one that best fits your purpose, your personality, and your budget.

chapter 7

Wall Coverings

*How to add excitement to your decorating scheme
with well-chosen, inexpensive wall coverings.*

If you want decorative walls that set the mood for the furnishings in a room, you have a wide choice of inexpensive materials from which to choose. Now homemakers do not have to be content merely to freshen walls with a new coat of paint in a bland color, or wallpaper in a vague, indistinct pattern. Whether you do the job yourself or hire a professional, you will find paint and other wall coverings to fit every room and every budget.

Walls can be decorated so that rooms appear larger or smaller and ceilings lower or higher. The proper wall treatment can magnify desirable architectural features, and minimize awkward or ugly ones; it can visually change the size and shape of a room. If you have furnishings that you want to spotlight, let the walls provide a subtle background shell. If you want the walls to be the dominant force, you can make them come alive with vibrant colors, exciting patterns, and unusual textures.

When planning for a new wall treatment, consider carefully the following areas. Is the room large or small? Is it light and airy, or dark and gloomy? Is wall space uncluttered, or is it cut up by doors and windows? Are there interesting architectural features that you want to emphasize, or outmoded or undesirable ones that you want to conceal? Will the new wall cover-

ing be part of a total room decorating project, or will it have to be compatible with other elements of the existing decor?

If you are a home owner, you may want to invest in a more expensive wall covering that will give long years of service and satisfaction. If you are a renter, there may be decorating limitations imposed by the landlord. And, last but not least, how much do you want to invest?

In addition to the familiar paint and wallpaper, there is a long list of wall coverings that includes fabrics and vinyl-coated materials, plastic laminates and vinyl tile, felt and leatherlike material—all in an inexpensive price range. Foils and flocked papers, painted murals, cork, ceramic tile, carpeting, wood shingles, brick, stone, wood veneers, and mirrors are more expensive, but still within the confines of the average budget if used only on one wall or as a panel. Most of these wall coverings are easy to care for and can be installed by the home handyman.

A handyman or homemaker can create an effect with wall coverings that is similar to the one used in the room at right. Cover a small wall with sale fabric or a large wall with only three or four panels of the fabric. Then, repeat the pattern and fabric in some other part of the room by making slipcovers, pillows, or a round table cloth.

COVER A WALL WITH PAINT

Paint is probably the most widely used wall covering because it is inexpensive and is easy and quick to apply. Even the most inexperienced novice can expect professional results if he tackles a paint job with confidence and follows the simple instructions outlined here. The right color of paint can visually change the dimensions of any room. Small rooms look larger if they are painted a light color and if the woodwork color matches the walls. A very large area appears smaller if it is painted a dark hue. All the walls need not be exactly the same color.

Create a similar one-tone theme in your home by having wall paint custom mixed to match a color in your drapery and upholstery fabrics.

TYPES OF PAINT

A multitude of colors ranging from the most subtle tints of neutrals all the way to deep and dramatic shades are available from your paint dealer. In addition to a large selection of ready-mixed paints, there are paints that can be custom-mixed to match fabrics, carpeting, and accessories.

Both latex and enamel paints, available in flat, semigloss or high-gloss finishes, work well on walls and ceilings. Latex is easier to apply because cleaning up afterward is less trouble and because you don't need to worry about lap marks. It also dries rapidly (two coats can be applied in a single day). Enamel makes a good finish, especially for bathrooms and kitchens, and holds up well under frequent scrubbings.

For painting woodwork, you may choose high-gloss, semigloss, or flat finishes in either enamel oil-base paint or latex water-base paint. The type of paint you choose once again depends on the amount of shine you want, where the paint will be used (water-base paints do not hold up as well as oil-base paints on areas which require frequent scrubbings), and how adept you are at painting (water-base paints are easier to apply, and clean-up time is less than with oil-base paints).

HOW TO PAINT A ROOM

Before you start, be sure that you have all the necessary equipment. In addition to the paint itself, you will need a drop cloth and wiping cloths, sandpaper and/or liquid sander, brushes, rollers, masking tape, patching plaster and a putty knife to fill any holes or cracks, a paint scraper to remove any build-up of old paint or varnish, thinner, and brush cleaner if you are using oil-base paint. Also, remember to read all instructions printed on the various products' containers carefully before actually getting to work.

A complete paint job would include woodwork, ceiling, and walls. If this is what you plan, do the woodwork first, the ceiling next, then the walls. If you are doing just the ceiling and walls, do the ceiling first, then the walls to avoid run marks and to ease clean-up.

If you decide to paint the woodwork, remove all doorplates and hardware first. If the woodwork has a sound surface of semigloss paint, you only need to use a liquid sander. This solvent removes wax and dirt and softens the surface of an old finish so that new paint will adhere to it. Use the liquid sander as you paint. Work ahead so that you paint the treated surface within half an hour or less. To be completely safe, use liquid sander first, then follow up with fine sandpaper (120 grit) until all traces of gloss are gone.

On woodwork that has previously been varnished, both liquid sander and hand sanding are necessary. If the woodwork is old and has been stained a dark color, test with a small amount of paint to see if the stain bleeds through. If it does, apply two coats of white shellac before painting. If there are blistered areas around the window frames and sills, use a paint scraper and then feather edges with 80-grit sandpaper. Do the same wherever there are chipped or damaged places.

If there are thick layers of old paint or varnish that have not been properly applied and the surface is in bad shape, sand and scrape down to the bare wood. If there are several layers of enamel, it may be necessary to use a wash-away type paint remover to do the job completely.

The most efficient way to paint woodwork is to use both a roller and a brush. Use a short-napped roller for all flat surfaces, and a brush for areas which can not be covered by the roller. When painting the baseboard, use a strip of cardboard placed next to the baseboard to protect the floor from splatters.

When you paint window trim, cover the areas that won't be painted with masking tape and use a sash brush (bristles are tapered and slant to one edge).

Before painting the ceiling and walls, remove all light fixtures, switch plate covers, and wall hangings, and patch wherever it may be necessary.

Use patching plaster and a putty knife to fill holes and mend cracked plaster. When the patching plaster is hard, sand the areas smooth. If the walls have crayon or grease marks, remove them with turpentine. Use a strong detergent to scrub any badly soiled areas. Protect the furnishings and floors with drop cloths and newspapers from around the house.

When painting the ceiling, attach a long extension to the handle of your paint roller so you can easily reach the ceiling.

When you are painting either walls or ceiling with a roller, move it in broad overlapping strokes. Use a small brush to paint in the corners. Whether you are painting walls, ceiling, or woodwork, the most important aspect is preparing the surface before you start applying the paint.

Dramatize a room's appearance with that coordinated fabric look—draperies that harmonize with adjoining wall coverings.

HOW TO WALLPAPER A ROOM

Whether you plan to paper an entire room, one wall, or hang a single panel, there are colors, patterns, and textures that will help to achieve the mood you desire. Wallpaper designs range from reproductions of museum wall hangings to bold and vivid creations of contemporary artists. From these you will find patterns that enhance furnishings of every style and ones that will complement any room in your home.

Along with its quality of adding drama to your decorating scheme, wallpaper is practical as well. Most of it is washable and easy to care for. Much of it is pre-pasted and pre-trimmed which simplifies hanging for the do-it-yourself homemaker. Some of it is strippable and can easily be removed when it is time for a change.

Prices vary according to design, quality, and type of paper. Even in the economy price range, there are interesting patterns that will maintain a fresh appearance for a number of years. If you have your heart set on a very costly wallpaper that will highlight the entire room, it still might not be a strain on the budget if you use it only on one wall. A wall ten feet wide and nine feet high will need just three single rolls. The average life of most wallpaper is six years. So, if it costs you $24 ($8 a roll) to cover the one wall, it really costs only $4 a year. That isn't very much money for such a dramatic effect.

If you are redecorating an entire room, you may want to choose wallpaper first, then build a color scheme around it. If it will have to harmonize with existing furnishings, take carpet, paint, and fabric samples with you and pick a pattern that is in harmony with your furnishings. Examine the wallpaper under both natural and artificial light as colors can vary.

Keep in mind that light colors make a room appear larger, while dark colors shrink a room. A wallpaper mural creates an optic illusion that visually pushes the walls away and makes even a small room look much larger.

Choose a pattern that is scaled to the size of the room. Occasionally, you might disregard this rule; that is, if you are try-ing to achieve a dramatic effect with the use of a very large, bold pattern on a single wall of a bathroom, bedroom, or hallway.

HOW TO MEASURE FOR WALLPAPER

Wallpaper is priced by the roll, and a roll contains 35 square feet. Narrow papers, between 18 and 20½ inches wide, come in double-bolt rolls. Wider papers, 28 inches, usually come in triple-bolts.

If you give your wallpaper sales person the measurements of the walls you want to cover and the dimensions of all the doors and windows, he will figure exactly how many rolls you will need. If you want to estimate it yourself, measure the length around your room in feet and multiply by the height from the ceiling to the baseboard. This will give the total number of square feet. Deduct the door and window space and any other openings. Divide the square feet by 30 for the number of single rolls you will need. Dividing by 30 instead of 35 allows a little extra for waste in matching the patterns.

Special characteristics of the wallpaper —whether it's washable, fadeproof, or plastic-coated—are printed on the back of every single roll.

HOW TO HANG WALLPAPER

If you plan to hang your own wallpaper, you will need a few simple tools. There are wallpaper kits that have a paste brush, plumb line, hard roller, and a smoothing brush. Other items—scissors, razor blade, bucket for paste, and sponge—you probably have around the house.

If there is old wallpaper that must be removed, you no longer need to scrape or steam it off. There is a roller that fits on a standard paint roller handle that will do the job. Simply dip the roller in warm, soapy water and roll it up and down the wall, soaking the paper thoroughly. There are ridges in the roller that perforate the old paper and drive water behind it to soften the paste. In about five minutes, a wall scraper will normally peel the paper off in large sheets.

Fill the cracks and holes with spackling

compound or patching plaster; when it is dry, sand it smooth. For a truly professional job, apply a coat of wall-sizing.

Getting the first strip properly aligned is the key to a successful job. In order to do this, drop a plumb line. Start at a doorway or in one corner of the room. Measure out to your right at the ceiling line to a distance one inch less than the width of the wallpaper and mark. Rub a piece of chalk on a string, hang a weight at one end, and fasten the other end to a tack at your mark. Let the weighted string down to establish a perfectly vertical line. Hold the string taut against the baseboard and snap the chalk line against the wall. The chalk mark will give an accurate vertical line for aligning the first strip.

Measure and cut the wallpaper to size on a flat surface or table. Unroll the paper, pattern side up, and pull gently but firmly across the edge of the table to remove the curl. Use scissors to cut the strips the height of the wall plus four inches to allow for matching and trimming. Match the pattern of each succeeding strip exactly at the right hand side of the preceding strip.

Some types of paper require special handling, or a particular kind of paste. Be sure to follow the manufacturer's recommendations included with each roll.

If you add a few drops of food coloring to the wallpaper paste, you can readily tell if the entire surface is covered. Brush the paste over half of the first strip, leaving an inch or two free of paste at the end. Fold the pasted end toward the center, without forming a crease. Slide the paper along the table and paste the paper carefully. If the paper is untrimmed, trim off the selvage at this time, using a razor blade and straightedge, if available.

Line up the right-hand edge of the paper with the chalk mark, letting the top edge of the paper extend about two inches above the ceiling line (excess will be trimmed later). Apply the top half of the strip to the wall by holding the unpasted edge with one hand and pulling the pasted fold apart.

When the paper is aligned, smooth it down with the smoothing brush, working from top to bottom. Repeat this process

One wall of striped wallpaper and matching drapery and upholstery fabric can be inexpensive if you can provide the labor yourself.

with the second half of the strip. Sponge off the excess paste before it dries so as to achieve a smooth surface.

Match patterns of each succeeding strip exactly at the right hand side of the preceding strip. Use a seam roller to roll down the joint between the two strips. Trim all excess paper at the ceiling and baseboard with a razor or knife before the adhesive dries. At the windows and doors, cut short strips from left-over strips of paper, carefully match the pattern to the adjacent strips already hung. Extend the wallpaper around corners at least a half inch.

HOW TO APPLY FABRIC TO WALLS

Applying fabric to walls is no longer the difficult task it once was because of the adhesives now available for this purpose. The same fabric used to cover walls, or a single wall, can be repeated in draperies, upholstered pieces, cushions, or bedspreads for a dramatic one-fabric splurge. Even an inexpensive patterned cotton, checked gingham, or a mattress ticking stripe can give the appearance of a professional, decorative treatment. Any fabric can be attached with liquid adhesive, hung with double-faced pressure sensitive tape, or stapled to the wall with a stapling gun.

There are also special fabric wall coverings with an adhesive backing. All you have to do is peel off the paper and press the fabric on the wall. Felt, burlap, grasscloth, and many other textures and weaves are available in this type of wall covering. These wall coverings are inexpensive if put on only one wall and are much easier to hang than other fabrics.

HOW TO PANEL WALLS

Today, the increasing popularity of low-cost factory-finished wood paneling has provided an incentive for building supply dealers to offer an even wider selection of natural wood colors, with molding and trim to match. Along with the beauty that warm, mellow wood tones add to a room, paneling requires a minimum of upkeep, offers long years of service, and the 4x8-foot prefinished panels are relatively easy to install as a do-it-yourself project.

There are natural wood grains and colors to suit any room, any mood, or any style of furnishings. It can be used for an entire room, a single wall, or simply a panel to provide accent to the rest of the room. Regardless of whether your home is old or new, or whether the walls are in good or poor condition, paneling offers the once-and-for-all solution to wall decorating. Baked-on finishes eliminate the need for further finishing and are literally guaranteed to last a lifetime.

A dimensional wall treatment, achieved by painting one wall and attaching inexpensive 16-inch wide hardboard panels, with epoxy cement or plastic resin glue, has a look of luxury.

It is possible to install paneling with a few hand tools, but using a power saw will speed up the operation. The prerequisites for a professional looking job are taking accurate measurements, using common sense, and making sure that edges are plumb or as close as you can get them.

The first step is to prepare the wall. Check it for plumb, and be certain there is no loose plaster or other irregularity. Then install furring strips. Generally, it is more desirable to use furring strips than to apply panels directly to an old wall.

Horizontal furring strips should be applied not more than 24 inches apart, and vertical strips every 16 inches or where panel joints occur. If the wall appears "hollow" in spots, level out the furring strips. Use cut steel nails or resin-coated nails to attach furring to plaster walls. If necessary, a moisture barrier should be applied to walls before you attach furring.

Next, lay out the job. Place the panels about the room to plan sequence for desired grain and color effects. For most interiors, it is wise to start in one corner and then work around the room.

The third step is the application of the panels. Many panels are manufactured with tongue-and-groove joints, so there is no difficulty in joining them. Others butt together and are prepared so they form a simple V-joint. (You can make a V-joint simply by running a plane along the edge of each panel before application.)

If paneling is to be attached with nails and edges concealed with molding, battens, or posts, common nails can be used. If nails will be exposed, use nails with heads colored to match finish surface. All nails should be applied ½ inch from outside edges, spaced 6 inches apart at top and bottom of panels and 12 inches apart on the vertical edges.

If paneling is to be applied with adhesive, be sure to follow the manufacturer's recommendations printed on the label. In addition, secure panels with a nail in each corner. Then hold panels in position with bracing until adhesive is set.

When all panels are in place, add matching ceiling and baseboard moldings.

Use three- to five-penny nails to fasten furring strips to studs. Use scrap pieces vertically to fill between strips at corners.

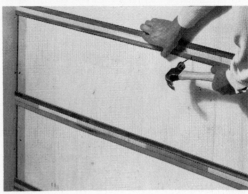

Insert clips into grooves, turning 90 degrees to lock in place. Fit flange of clip over lip of plank. If it is snug, tap with claw hammer.

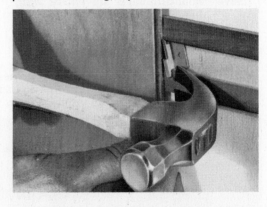

Next, slip planks into place so that clips engage bottom lip of plank. Top lip conceals clips, forming V-joint with other plank.

cover a wall with your own idea

Even in a room that is sparsely furnished or one that is drab and colorless, a lively wall treatment can revitalize the entire room. It can enhance and accent furnishings you are proud to display, or it can dominate a room so that items you wish to ignore will fade into obscurity.

If you are searching for an idea that will add individuality and color to a bare stretch of wall—and one that is economical—perhaps the following suggestions will help you a little.

Fabric panels. One of the most effective wall treatments is achieved through the use of fabric panels. Fabric panels are simple and quick to apply, and they are inexpensive. You can cover an entire wall, hang a panel from ceiling to floor, or simply use a large piece of fabric that is interesting enough to serve as a substitute for a costly original painting. Your choice depends on the size of your room, and how forceful you want this portion of your decorating plan to appear.

If you cover the whole wall or hang a floor-to-ceiling panel, you should choose fabric that is used elsewhere in the room. Repeat the drapery or upholstery fabric for a coordinated look. Stripes, florals, geometrics, documentary prints, and plaids are all suitable.

If you want to hang a piece of fabric to decorate a wall just as a painting would, search in the drapery and fabric departments for a remnant or sample. These are usually sold at a fraction of the per-yard cost of full bolts. Choose a large, dramatic pattern and colors that harmonize with

Solid oak parquet flooring comes in nine-inch squares and is laid in alternate-grain patterns and applied with tile cement. This treatment is an inexpensive solution for covering a scarred wall.

Create an atmosphere of an outdoor dining area inside by using a lattice-work patterned wallpaper on one wall and as a border.

Add a touch of elegance to any wall in your home inexpensively by watching for odd-lot or discontinued pattern sales on wallpaper.

your decor: a bold abstract or geometric print, or a realistic scenic pattern.

There are cottons, linens, rayons, and blends in various finishes and textures. For extra durability, try striped mattress ticking. For ease of application and removal when it is time for a change, attach panels to the wall with double-faced pressure-sensitive tape. Be sure to hold material taut when you are fastening it so that it will have a smooth appearance. If you hang a single panel, outline it with a vinyl tape border. By doing this, it will look like a frame. To increase soil resistance, spray the fabric with a clear lacquer after hanging and let it dry very well.

Felt, too, makes a good wall covering. It is inexpensive, is easy to work with (72-

inch widths), and is available in a wide variety of colors.

If you are part of the mobile society and must move to a new location frequently, you can move your decorative walls with you. There are murals, mounted on a hardboard backing, that can either hang from hooks attached to the ceiling, or fasten to suspension poles that extend from ceiling to floor. If the mural hangs very close to the wall, it looks like a part of the room; if it is mounted elsewhere, it can serve as a divider wall. When the time comes to move, take the mural along with you and rehang it in your new home.

Motifs. Another way to liven up a neutral painted wall is to cut out large fabric or wallpaper motifs and apply them to the wall with adhesive. Try several arrangements before you actually glue them to the wall so that the finished grouping is one that pleases you, and complements the rest of your room and its furnishings.

Borders. Another way to add interest to an ordinary wall is to use stenciled borders and designs. You can buy stencils, or you can make your own. Fasten the stencil to the wall securely with masking tape and use a stencil brush to paint in the design. When you remove the stencil, be careful not to smear the wet paint. The same stencil designs or borders that you use on walls can also be used to decorate window shades or painted furniture.

Tile. There are many types of tiles on the market today that you can use as decorative wall coverings. These cover a wide price range, but even the more ex-

pensive offerings can be used in a small area and produce an exciting decorative effect without too great an expenditure.

There are metal wall tiles of gleaming solid copper, solid stainless steel, and several aluminum finishes. These come in 4¼-inch square sizes and have built-in adhesive areas inside each corner. These can be put up in minutes. There are also simulated tile or stone squares that have a self-sticking back. Indoor-outdoor carpet tiles that come in 12-inch squares can be applied to a wall with double-faced tape or a special adhesive. These can be laid full-size, or cut with a knife for designing unique motifs. Ceramic tiles, or less expensive plastic tiles, come in 4¼-inch standard size squares. These are installed by cementing to the wall, and finished by grouting. Mirror tiles in regular or antique

Paint one wall bright red. Next, paint a 4x8-foot sheet of hardboard white. When dry, lay it out flat and apply a pattern of black vinyl cloth tape, cut in several widths. Paint in large black areas with tempera. Using plywood, make one long box for the shelf and three small ones for supports. Paint the shelf white and screw to the wall.

finishes add spaciousness to any room. They have a rubberized backing for easy handling. Be sure to use mirror mastic to attach these sheets to the wall, as other adhesives might possibly damage the mirror's silvering.

Cork makes an interesting wall covering, and comes in either 9-inch squares or in large sheets. There are red cedar shakes and shingles that add a touch of the outdoors to either a contemporary or traditional setting. They can be stained a broad range of wood tones or decorator colors. Since they are applied individually, you can arrange color tones and textural effects however you wish.

Fiber glass panels. These simulate the look of natural materials—brick, stone, or barn siding—and come in 4x8-foot sheets, with a nailing lip around the edge for easy installation. For a brick wall that doesn't require a mason's skill, there is real kiln-fired brick, that is only ¼ inch thick. This is perfect for any wall where you want the beauty of brick, but don't need the structural strength. Use mastic and install just as you would tile.

Hardboard. This comes in random-grooved, plastic-finished 4x8-foot sheets and is simple to install. It is easy to clean, conceals old cracked plaster, and is easily applied to walls with finishing nails.

Bamboo. For a basement recreation room, use bamboo for a wall covering that gives a year-round outdoor atmosphere. First, paint the wall with a below-grade paint. Use bamboo that has the strips woven with galvanized wire and comes in a 15-foot roll, 6 feet high. Unroll the bamboo as you go along, securing it to the wall here and there with concrete nails. Use an extra piece of the bamboo at the base to act as a molding.

Linoleum. To brighten up a cheerless basement laundry room, or a playroom, choose linoleum in a bright color and use it on both walls and floors. Linoleum comes in both 9- and 12-foot widths; use plastic stripping to hide seams.

Vinyls. There are a large number of vinyls in a wide range of colors and patterns that are excellent materials for wall coverings. There are foam-, fabric-, and foil-backed vinyls, and plastic vinyls. They are washable, waterproof, and easy to apply. Plastic vinyl has a self-adhesive backing, so all you have to do is cut to fit, peel off backing, press down, and smooth out. Smoothly polished foam-backed vinyl conceals wall defects and irregularities, and has a sound deadening quality, too. To install, stretch one panel on the wall at a time—tacking lightly for temporary holding. Fold back a wide edge, and apply adhesive, then press firmly to the wall. Do this on all four sides. Remove tacks when adhesive has dried. Use a decorative band or molding to cover seams. Foil vinyl can be installed in the same way as wallpaper, or you can get it with the self-adhesive backing at most wallpaper stores.

Decorator tape. Vinyl-coated cloth decorator tape adds zest to a humdrum painted wall. In a child's room with walls painted white, try alternate stripes of red and blue tape; in a breakfast room, you might like orange and yellow. Tape, in ¾- or 2-inch widths, comes in decorator colors with an adhesive backing; you simply press it on the wall. When it is time for redecorating, just peel it off. Create your own patterns: stripes, plaids, or grillwork designs with this easy-on tape.

Personalized ideas. There are also many uses for personal items: if you are a sailing enthusiast, you can paper a wall with navigation charts; a small child might like circus posters; a teenager, record jackets featuring his favorite recording artists; a music student might like sheet music; a little theater group member, theater programs; one who likes to travel, maps or travel posters; and a gourmet, menu covers. (There was even a budding journalist who papered a closet wall with rejection slips from publishers.)

New materials suitable for use as wall coverings appear daily. Watch for announcements in newspapers and magazines when new products appear. Make occasional trips to decorating shops, paint and wallpaper departments, and building supply dealers. Make your walls an important part of your total decor.

chapter 8

Finding & Arranging Accessories

Accessories—the one area where your imagination can run rampant without being concerned with function.

An accessory is like the icing on a cake. It is decorative, but not necessarily functional. This is the one area of home furnishings that does not require you to be concerned with practical aspects. If an accessory adds beauty to a room, this is really all that matters.

For example, you may choose to display a rock on your coffee table. As long as it adds beauty to the room through color, texture, form, or balance—and it pleases you—it need not have any other purpose. It is perfectly alright to use it as a paperweight or a wishing stone but, by its own right, it can simply rest there and be nothing but a decorative accessory.

Accessories can be as costly or as inexpensive as your budget allows, and they should be given as much consideration as the other furnishings in the home. Often it is merely displaying to advantage those furnishings you already have.

Accessories may be purely decorative, such as paintings, sculpture, wood carvings, greenery, and many types of collectibles, or they may be useful as well as decorative. In the latter category, there are clocks, bowls for flowers or fruit, vases, ash trays, candlesticks, and mirrors.

Keep in mind that this is the one area of decorating that allows you to give your home the stamp of individuality. Many homes may have similar pieces of furniture; some radiate warmth and charm, others seem drab and ordinary. It is the choice of accessories and how they are arranged that makes one home different from another. Accessories afford an ideal outlet for revealing the personalities, interests, and hobbies of the occupants. It isn't the amount of money you spend on accessories that is important. Rather, it is using your imagination to add an unusual touch that gives your room that extra sparkle.

In the room at right, varied sizes and shapes of accessories are well balanced to create harmony out of diversity. The secret of grouping a miscellaneous assemblage like this is to concentrate on total effect, rather than the pallid use of one or two elements. A collection of prints and personal bibelots make up the interesting wall arrangement; the sofa pillows, tiger skin rug, flowering plant, and other table accessories add unity to the total arrangement. The sofa and other furniture pieces provide the solid base needed to support the arrangement.

how to display accessories

Accessory arrangement can be haphazard —an art object placed here, two or three pictures placed there, a cushion thrown on a sofa where it may be sat on or used as a headrest, a whole mass of small or large china pieces grouped on a small table—or it can be exciting and artfully designed adding to the room's decorating scheme.

Break away from your old habits. Plan your accessories so they complement your ideas in decorating. Find a niche or an unusual spot to accessorize. Fit them into your kitchen plan. Place them in your laundry room. Select a dull corner in a passageway and brighten it with a blend of colorful accessories. Use accessories to add drama and function to each room, each small corner in your home. And do it tastefully and with a scheme in mind. Accessories supply that extra "something" making an ordinary room into a unique living area.

No matter how tiny a room is, make space for accessories. Fill the niches with accessories appropriate to the room and the person who occupies that room. This room obviously belongs to a photography buff. The space along the ceiling makes a perfect place to display his prints.

HOW TO PLAN A WALL GROUPING

A wall is a good place to put to practice your new-found nerve for accessorizing. You can turn every wall in your home into a memory bank, and, if you study our example, you can do this with next to no cost.

Not everybody starts out with a collection of original art or an interesting group of pictures. You achieve each piece individually. With a small selection to work with, you may feel there isn't enough, but there are many ways to achieve an interesting wall grouping. A fabric panel, a travel poster, or a large map simply framed with four slim pieces of wood can fill a decorative void today, and can be replaced when you acquire something more desirable. In short, you don't have to buy an expensive original print to fill up the dining room wall. You may not even like an original print. But if you do, you can fill up the wall now and buy a high-priced item when your budget allows.

If you want to learn the art of accessory display, choose a wall to practice on—a large wall. Think in terms of scale, unity, and balance and combine pictures or framed accessories of various sizes. Then stand back. Is the group too close together? Conversely, are the hangings too far apart? If nothing seems right, go back to the trusty decorating method—sketch out your framings according to scale and fit them onto a scaled-out piece of paper. Once you have decided on a plan, draw it on a large sheet of paper. Then, trace around each object to full-scale and attach these sheets of paper to the walls.

If nothing seems to work, don't despair. Cheat a little. Copy the wall arrangements that you will find in any good home furnishings magazine or book. The design you select and use will grow on you; before you are aware of it, you will have grasped the essentials of good arrangement and will be ready to start on another wall— this time using your own ideas.

A permanent accessory, such as a lamp, clock, or the sconce in this informal dining area, can launch an arrangement. Group prints around it and add fruit and vegetable plaques to supply dimension and interest.

Create your own family portrait gallery. When you want to use photos of the children, don't be shy. Combine a number of shots and group them in one large display. Use them in a niche under the stairs.

WHICH FASTENERS TO USE

In order to hang any accessory, you must know the type of wall construction, what type of hardware is required, what tools to use, and the exact position you want.

When hanging objects that weigh less than 20 pounds on plaster or sheet rock walls, use angled picture hooks. Since plaster chips easily, hammer lightly and attach a small piece of scotch tape to the wall for protection. Place the hook over the scotch tape and pound it gently through the tape, avoiding cracking the plaster.

For wood paneled walls, use the same procedure, but omit the tape, and substitute wood screws for the picture hooks. When hanging objects of less than 20 pounds on brick or masonry walls, use steel-cut nails. Be careful to hammer them into the mortar so that the bricks or pieces of stone do not chip.

If you are hanging lightweight pictures, use steel sewing needles rather than picture hangers. These will support more weight than you realize and will leave no visible hole in the wall. Hold them in a slanting position, and tap gently into the wall with a hammer. If you are mounting

fabric panels, maps, or posters on the wall, use double-faced pressure sensitive tape. This makes them easy to hang, and also easy to remove when you desire a change.

Objects weighing more than 20 pounds should be secured to the wall studding. Locating the studding is not always easy, but you can usually tell by tapping along the wall until the tap sounds more like a solid thump. There is also a small gadget on the market whose magnet will be drawn toward the nails in the studs if you move it along the wall at the baseboard. Studs are usually spaced 16 inches apart on center, but this is not always the case with every single building.

If you are hanging objects that weigh more than 20 pounds on brick or stone walls, drill a hole into the brick or stone and use lead expansion shields as a substitution for picture hooks.

Shelves with bracket arm supports are hung in two ways. The best way is to secure the strips directly to the studs with wood screws. When a shelf must hang in a certain spot and there are no studs, use toggle bolts if the wall is plastered and molly bolts if covered with sheet rock.

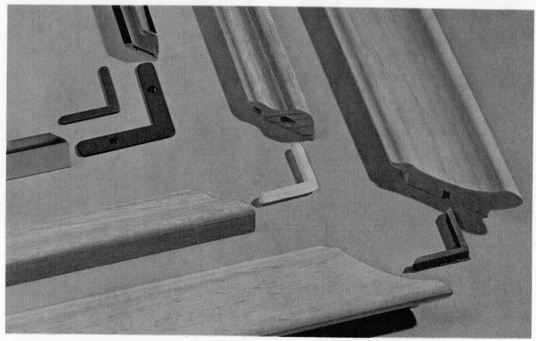

The frames above are available in both wood and metal, in lengths to fit your most common needs. Since they come with the corners already mitered, you simply tap them together and glue, if necessary. For an unusual frame, use one fitted inside the other.

HOW TO MAKE PICTURE FRAMES

Picture frames can be inexpensive if you learn how to make your own.

Most building supply dealers carry a good selection of builder's moldings that can be used singly, or in combination, to create almost any design of picture frame. It doesn't take a lot of tools, but a miter box-corner clamp will make the job much easier for you to accomplish.

Cut the frame pieces on a 45-degree angle so that you will have perfectly mitered corners. Put a rabbet (a groove into which the picture will fit) in the back of the frame. An oil painting, which requires no glass, is tacked to a narrow wood frame that fits into the rabbet. If you are framing a picture that will be matted and covered with glass, the depth of the rabbet must be adjusted to ensure accommodation of all three thicknesses.

Glue the frame sections together and use clamps to hold them securely until the glue is thoroughly dry. However, use glue sparingly so that none of it remains on the surface. Otherwise, this will prevent the stain from penetrating—when it causes a very noticeable white spot.

Frames can be finished with paints, metallic finishes, or stains and varnish. For a distressed or antique finish, tap on the completed frame lightly with a hammer or sharp object. Then, sand the surface lightly to remove any splinters, and apply the required finish.

Usually, matted, glass-covered pictures have narrower frames than do oil paintings. The mat acts as an extension of the frame, and together they resemble a wide frame. The mat also prevents moisture from the glass touching the picture. Mat board is available in a wide range of colors at most art supply shops. Use a sharp mat knife to cut mat board; always be sure to leave a slightly wider border at the bottom edge of the mat than at the top edge.

THREE-DIMENSIONAL ACCESSORIES

In addition to flat wall groupings, you can add drama to your room with dramatic three-dimensional accessories. Mirrors of all sizes unframed or with simple or ornate frames; clocks, old or new, in wood, metal, crystal, or porcelain finishes; pillows, in a wide variety of colors and shapes; and greenery, small potted plants or small trees, add warmth and individual personality to any room.

There are no rules of thumb to guide the choice of "correct" accessories, but there are some general principles that can help you in the selection, and ways of displaying three-dimensional decorations so they will be in harmony with the setting you give them.

Most important, of course, is to decide whether or not you really like the particular item in question. If it doesn't please you in and of itself, don't choose it merely because it will go with your decorating scheme. A cut glass accessory placed in the center of your sideboard may fit into the decorating scheme, but if you don't like it, it is next to useless as an accessory in your home. Continue your search until you find the item that both meets your decorating needs and pleases your senses.

Once the items are chosen, consider the way to display them most attractively. Do you want a symmetrical arrangement or an asymmetrical one? Will the objects be grouped or will they be shown singly? These are some of the facts that you need to take into consideration.

Also consider what you want the accessory or accessories to do. Are they to be pleasing but nonfunctional items—a collection of butterflies, mounted and framed, designed to show your interest in Lepidopterology? Or, will the accessory also serve a useful purpose? For there are many decorating possibilities for any accessory.

Although you may have never thought of it in this way, the most common device for simulating height is through the use of decorative accessories—groupings of ornamental objects, single tall mirrors, tall ferns and, even, ceiling-hung light fixtures —that can give the appearance of height to a small room. This is best achieved by placing the item above the level of low pieces of furniture as the accessory serves to carry the eye above the furniture, creating an illusion of height.

You can also use accessories to achieve an illusion of length. Try an entire wall of plants. Place a tall house tree in one corner and a series of smaller plants, ranging downward in size, so that the smallest plant is in the adjacent corner.

Three dimensional accessories can also color coordinate your room. Select accessories whose color is repeated in your walls or draperies and place them in the center of the room or on a sofa. It may be a jewelled box, an ivory tusk, a small collection of coins, an ashtray, a tall slender vase, or a single-color pillow that complements the room's color scheme.

Whatever the reason for your choice of accessory, an accessory can add both to your enjoyment and to the decorating scheme of the room.

You can convert a dull wall into a room's focal point with a group of shelves that hold prized possessions, and a few framed prints. Shelves provide many opportunities for the imaginative and creative decorator.

LIGHTING AS AN ACCESSORY

Good lighting encompasses two important functions. It should supply the proper amount and type of light for specific tasks and leisure-time activities, and it should also add beauty to the colors and furnishings in your home.

There are three significant types of lighting in every well-planned home: background, or general lighting; local; and accent. It takes all three, correctly positioned, to provide balanced illumination.

Background, or general lighting, provides a room with soft general illumination. It comes from ceiling or wall fixtures, luminous ceilings and panels, cornice lighting, or reflected light from any source.

Local light is necessary for reading, sewing, card playing, hobby activities, and many other pastimes, and should be used along with good general lighting. Local light can be supplied by table or floor lamps or by suspended ceiling fixtures.

Build a hanging fixture with four pieces of 9x12½-inch plastic and a 9-inch square top piece. Butt joints and glue. Drill a hole for the cord and glue cork on the sides.

TYPES OF LIGHTING FIXTURES

The selection of lighting fixtures is constantly expanding; there are designs to complement all furniture styles. Basically, there are three major categories: ceiling fixtures, lamps, and wall lights. Each category has its own characteristics.

Ceiling fixtures are mounted close to the ceiling, suspended from it by a chain or cord, or fitted above the ceiling behind a flush translucent panel. Lamps include table, floor, and swag lamps. Wall lights include wall lamps, cornice, valance, and bracket fixtures. Cornice and valance lights are installed above curtains or draperies; brackets may be mounted anywhere.

In a dining room, use low level, general illumination to create a serene atmosphere. A pull-down fixture with a dimmer switch offers complete flexibility for creating the mood that pleases you.

In bedrooms, you need good general illumination, plus bedside lamps for reading. In children's rooms, it is especially important to have adequate lighting for studying purposes.

Bathrooms should have both general and local lighting to make personal grooming chores easier for everyone concerned.

Kitchens, too, should have both general and local lighting. The ceiling fixture should be planned to furnish 150 to 200 watts incandescence, or 60 to 80 watts fluorescence for each 50 square feet of space. In addition, there should be fixtures installed under cabinets and above work centers. If the kitchen has large areas of deep-toned wood cabinets and paneling, or has little natural light, the artificial light output must be increased from the average figure quoted above. Incandescent bulbs may be either clear, white, or colored. If you use colored bulbs for reading or sewing, select the next higher wattage than recommended for white bulbs. Fluorescent tubes are either warm or cool. Warm white tubes enhance furnishings, blend well with incandescent lighting, and are also a good choice for bathrooms, where faces undergo close scrutiny. Cool white tubes create a cool atmosphere in a room that features cool shades of greens and blues.

PLANNING LIGHTING

Lighting should be even and well balanced. This means that it takes some planning for it to be efficient as well as to add beauty to your home and furnishings.

Accent lighting is just what its name implies. It is used purely to highlight important furniture groupings, wall hangings, or other accessories.

In order for your lighting to be effective, there must be sufficient circuits: three for general use, two each for kitchen, laundry, and dining areas, and one for each major appliance such as the washer and dryer.

There should also be a sufficient number of outlets for every room, two for every 12-foot wall, one for each major appliance, one for every four feet of wall in the kitchen, and at least one outlet near the bathroom mirror.

HOW TO BUY THE RIGHT LAMP

Lamps should combine both beauty and function. They should act as a decorative accent both day and night, as well as serve their primary role after dark.

Table lamps should be scaled to the size of the table or desk where they will be placed, and they should cast their light on the work surface. The table height plus the lamp base height should total between 39 and 42 inches for proper reading light. For desk work, the bottom of the shade should be 15 inches from the desk top.

If you need local light in a spot that will not accommodate a table, use a floor lamp or swag lighting fixture. Floor lamps take up very little floor space, and can easily be moved. Swag lamps can be positioned simply by installing hooks in the ceiling in the desired location.

The lamp below is low enough for adequate lighting, and also harmonizes with the lightly scaled furniture and decorative accessories.

Neither the lamp nor table is suitable for the chair. The lamp is too tall, and both tend to overpower the most important piece.

BUILD YOUR OWN SPECIAL-EFFECTS LIGHTING

You can add beauty and function to a room with the addition of a special lighting effect. While it is usually an expensive item, the added beauty and function it brings makes its installation worthwhile.

Valance, the most popular type of wall lighting, is always used above a window. The unit is placed above the draperies with the fluorescent tube positioned at the top of the valance faceboard, but not so high or far back that the fluorescent tube doesn't shine in front of the drapery.

Bracket units are a variation of a valance and are fitted onto a wall so light will flow up and down. Position the tube close to the wall so light flows up and down.

Cornice lighting directs all its light downward. Install the unit at the junction of the wall and the ceiling. Set the faceboard at least six inches from the wall and make it at least six inches deep.

For all three of these lighting installations, paint the inside of the faceboard white to obtain the best reflection.

For a dramatic effect, highlight cabinets and shelves with fluorescent lighting. Or, install frosted glass shelves for a luminous effect. Or, use local lighting inside glass-topped bookshelves. A luminous wall unit makes a good backdrop to display greenery. Try general light under a window to spotlight the garden at night.

Coves, ceiling lighting used in small rooms or in alcoves with high ceilings, are either made of wood, metal, or plaster and should always be at least 12 inches below the ceiling with the light centered 4½ inches off the wall.

Luminous lighting consists of fluorescent tubes concealed above a ceiling of plastic panels. Paint ceiling cavity flat white for best light reflection. Packaged units, ready to assemble, can be purchased. They include channels, flexible plastic, and hardware. Installation is very simple.

A floating canopy is installed below ceiling height and over a particular section of a room you wish to highlight.

Coffer lighting is a cove bent into a circle or oval, and set into the ceiling.

The strategically placed cornice below has louvered plastic diffusers that conceal the light source from the conversation area.

Make a lamp base by fastening together with epoxy glue three 8½-inch clay flower pots and secure to a wooden block base.

Let lighting accessorize your room. The valance light in this bedroom casts a soft glow of light on the semisheer draperies, creating a soothing, atmosphere conducive to sleep.

You can use any one of several built-in lighting ideas. Above, three treatments—wall bracket, shelves, and panel of light—work harmoniously as one.

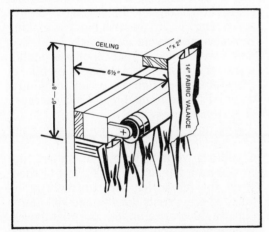

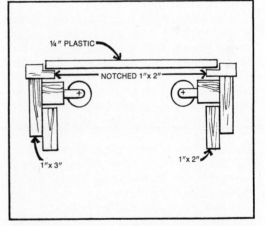

Build a valance from plywood or put the existing drapery valance to work for this decorative touch. To get even upward distribution of light and avoid an unpleasant hot streak on the ceiling, do one of the following with the shielding material: mount it at least ten inches from the ceiling or close it off at top. Shielding should be at least six inches wide; the tube at least two inches out from drapery.

In order for wall bracket to direct light up and down, allow at least three inches between wall and tube, and two inches between tube and shielding board. Build shelves deep enough to accommodate a fluorescent tube, and recess plastic inserts even with top. Put panel in stereo cabinet; make light box at least six inches deep and center a single fluorescent tube toward top. Recess a plastic panel level with top.

where to find accessories

Finding the accessory that will add sparkle to a room is oftentimes easier than you think. In addition to giftware and houseware departments and art galleries or antique stores, there is one source that will often provide you with all the accessories you need—your home.

Explore the attic; make an exhaustive search of closets, cupboards and drawers; work through the garage; if you have one, sift through the basement and check all old and new family albums—in each of these areas you will find small and large items that will readily fit into your accessorizing plan. Wedding gifts, bridge prizes, family hand-me-downs or family heirlooms that you had forgotten you had, photographs of family members past and present, crewel work or sewing projects done years ago by a senior member of the family and placed in a back drawer to be forgotten are all valuable accessories that you can use to good advantage in accessorizing your house or apartment.

The same holds true for hobby items. Collections of figurines, crystal, coins, menu covers, buttons, lead soldiers, butterflies, or sporting medals and ribbons are all suitable for framing when they are mounted on a wall or arranged as a three-dimensional display on a shelf. And whether it's a collection of antique cutglass, paperweights, cookie cutters, or lead soldiers, display them to advantage. If your hobby is photography, weaving, ceramics, or embroidery, use these hobby items in your home. Also, find room to show off your children's arts and crafts projects.

Unless you have a yen for expensive antiques or pieces of art, there is no need to forage in antique shops or to hunt in art galleries. You will probably be able to pick up momentoes of trips, vacations, or nature walks that double as reminders of your trip and serve as accessories.

If you have momentoes of trips—wood carvings, foreign coins, pottery, hand-woven fabrics, picture post cards, menus, rail or airline tickets—use them to create a wall of reminders. Mount them on cloth covered board and frame them. If you can't decide what to do with an assortment of foreign coins, inlay them in grout on a shallow metal plate and turn this into a mosaic ash tray of your own design.

In your search for memorable accessories, don't overlook the family nature walks or the garden. Scattered along your path are a myriad of small items that will brighten even the darkest area of your home. Milkweed pods, cattails, dried stalks of weeds and grains, flowers, or russet-colored stalks of corn can be turned into an accessory that will delight you and that will fit into any decorating scheme.

In your search for inexpensive accessories, don't forget any make-yourself items. For those who enjoy needlework, there is an endless variety of items that can be used to accessorize your home. Try a pillow or wall hanging with crewel design, a cross-stitch sampler, or a hooked or rya accent rug. Or, if you are a hand at making ceramics, make your own bowls, ash trays, and vases. And if your hobby is metalwork, try a wire sculpture, a mobile of graceful copper figures, or an aluminum tray. All these items fit into the category of *personal* accessories.

You may want to add to your personal accessories with items you buy. If so, and if you are working to a tight budget and cannot afford an art dealer's prices or those of an antique dealer, turn to the local art fairs. There, artists display and sell paintings, sculpture, ceramics, and metalwork. Who knows, the work you buy from a struggling artist today may be a collector's item sometime in the future.

Above all, in your search for accessories, always keep in mind that the item you select should be based on what you want to have in your home and not on what you think is "right". Take your time, shop around a bit, and you will soon find the accessory you want.

The warm, mellow gleam of copper is combined with books and a collection of various-sized pictures to create an interesting wall arrangement for this country-style kitchen dining area.

GUIDELINES TO FOLLOW

A successful arrangement is easy to accomplish if you follow these basic rules:

1. Hang most accessories at eye level or below. If the object is most often viewed from a seated position, hang the accessory at your seated eye level.
2. Exercise judgment in spacing accessories. When things are crowded together, nothing stands out, so add space between large objects.
3. Have one outstanding wall arrangement as your focal point.
4. Decorate every room in the house, including the often neglected hall, stairway, foyer, and bathroom.
5. For added interest, place some accessories in unexpected places. Try a picture hung on the ceiling or a poster at the bottom of the basement stairs.
6. Don't go overboard! Create a lived-in look without making the room appear crowded and confusing.
7. When using small objects, either on a wall or a table, arrange them in groups or clusters, and not in a row.
8. Use three-dimensional objects for variety and depth. Clocks, mirrors, plants, plaques, and shelves give needed height or length to a room.

chapter 9

Decorating Tips For Limited Budgets

How to make the most of your time, energy, and money with do-it-yourself decorating ideas under $100.

In the previous chapters we provided you with the elements of design—line, form, space, color, and texture—in relation to interior design. These chapters spelled out what constitutes good decorating and how all of these principles apply to your decorating. The preceding pages presented how easy it is to use color to your advantage, how to create space through furniture arrangement, how to add interest to walls, windows, and floors, and how to save, and invest when purchasing furnishings.

After familiarizing yourself with this important information, you're now ready to try your wings. You're now ready to apply these principles to your home. This chapter contains hundreds of do-it-yourself decorating ideas to use in your home. It contains projects you can build, sew, paint, and paste—all for $100 or less.

When you see an idea that particularly appeals to you, tackle the project courageously and enthusiastically. You don't have to be married to Mr. Fix-it or have a complete workshop in the basement. All that's really required is confidence, imagination, and a spirit of adventure.

From start to finish, maintain a positive attitude. Whatever you do, don't begin with the idea, "Gee, I wish I could do that, but I can't even hammer a nail in straight." You'll be amazed at what you can do now. Just don't be timid about asking for advice. You may not know a 2x4 piece of pine from a piece of plywood, but you can bet there will be more than one person in the lumber company who is qualified to answer your questions and who will be glad to help you if you will just ask questions as you purchase the materials needed for a project. The same applies to hardware stores and fabric shops.

For example, even if you've never held a hammer before, you can build this ceiling-high bookcase unit. To make it even easier, most lumber companies will cut the lumber for you. Use rough-sawn 2x10s and distress them with an axe or chisel. The more hacking and gouging you do, the more weathered they will look. Next stain the boards a dark walnut and seal with a satin-finish varnish. Partially drive two 6-inch nails into the top of each board. Remove the heads from the nails and ease the uprights into matching holes that were drilled into the ceiling. Enamel 1x10 pine shelving and secure the finished shelves with 3-inch lag screws.

tables on a limited budget

If you've found yourself a little short on tables, money, and time, here are some ideas just for you! They indicate that money isn't everything when it comes to decorating—ingenuity speaks louder.

The trick to stretching your furnishings dollars is to use costly materials in small areas but with big impact. Often, you can get dramatic effects by concentrating color, pattern, and design in a very small space. And, by using it only in a small space, you will be using only a small amount of expensive material.

Resourcefulness is the key to success. Open your eyes and look around you. Inexpensive table materials are all around.

Make an end table by clustering four orange crates, painting them with enamel, and trimming the top and side edges with upholstery tacks. Or, glue a sturdily framed butterfly collection to the top of a canvas camping stool. Also, cover an inexpensive, unfinished Parson's table with brightly colored contact paper.

If you have time some lazy afternoon, go on a scavenger hunt through the attic, the basement, and the second-hand shops. Don't just look for things that are tables already. Look for a pair of round swivel piano stools. You can spray paint them and use them as bunching tables in front of your sofa. Or, transform an old metal trunk into a cocktail table for the family room by gluing pictures, maps, or old sheet music all over it and then spraying several coats of lacquer on the entire surface. If you're really lucky and imaginative besides, perhaps you will find an old base drum. If you do, take it home and make a top for it from a circle of plywood. Paint or antique it and you'll be the envy of everyone on the block!

All projects are easy on both your budget and your time. But no matter what your next project may be, look in hobby shops, department stores, and lumber companies for new materials, products, and techniques that will make the job easier.

Make your own dining table from $1.50 cardboard clothes hampers from the dry cleaners, strips of wallpaper, and a slab door.

If you have enough olive oil cans, any old table can be a work of art. Just pound them out and tack them down with brass nails.

A cube has an infinite number of decorative possibilities. After you make a cube table from ¾-inch plywood, the magic of transformation begins. Cover five sides with 16x18 sheets of mirror squares attached with mirror mastic. And finish the side edges with a stainless steel rim.

With pressure-sensitive wallpaper, you can quickly transform an ordinary 18-inch cube into an elegant extra table. First, shellac the cube's raw wood surface. Then, cut the wallpaper into 6x6-inch squares. Apply the squares in an alternating design as shown in the top right illustration.

Or, to make the cube look like a block of wood, use iron-on plastic laminate wood grain paper. With the iron set on the cotton setting, press the laminate on the cube. Then, wipe the entire surface with a damp cloth to cool the adhesive.

screens and room dividers

Screens and room dividers play an important role in the open-plan theme of most of today's apartments and small houses. In these small living units, walls are often omitted between the kitchen and informal dining area, the living area and dining area, and the living area and entry. This is done partially to cut down on the building costs and also to keep a small floor plan from looking like a series of tiny interconnected boxlike rooms.

However, there are also areas where *you* might want partial privacy or, at least, separation. If so, use a floor-to-ceiling or ceiling-to-countertop divider to create a foyer to screen traffic from the living room, or to separate the dining area from the kitchen or living room. You can also use dividers to hide an untidy workbench, sewing center, or laundry area.

A folding screen which has three or more rigid panels hinged together is used in much the same way as room dividers; to divide space, to separate areas of activity, and to conceal work areas. Folding screens also have another function. When a room has no outstanding architectural focal point, a decorative screen used in combination with a small furniture grouping is often used to fill the void, and this screen and furniture grouping then becomes the focal point of the room.

No matter how you decorate your home-office work area, there are bound to be times when this area makes the rest of the room look messy. Solution: screen it off with a venetian blind.

Use a tall folding screen made of wooden panels to separate the living area from the entryway. Attach triangular plywood shelves to the panels and you have a great place to display accessories.

If for some reason you can't hang pictures on the walls, place a screen behind the sofa and hang your picture grouping on it with small picture-hanging tacks.

A decorative screen may be used as the focal point of the room and, at the same time, conceal a badly marred wall or poor architectural feature.

do-it-yourself dividers

With some imagination and very little money, you can build your own room dividers and screens. For almost any type of room divider you can imagine, there are materials readily available: some you may be able to salvage from buildings that are being demolished; others you may have to purchase at department stores and building supply companies.

One of the quickest, easiest, and most inexpensive ways to build a room divider is to use one or more panels of fabric. If the fabric comes in very wide widths, stretch one large panel from the floor to the ceiling. Nail or glue a 1x2-inch strip of wood to the ceiling and tack the fabric to it. Next, hem the bottom of the fabric, forming a casing and slip a metal rod through the casing so that the fabric is weighted. If the fabric is narrow, hang several strips with space between them.

If you move from place to place frequently or like to rearrange the furniture often, build mobile room dividers. One such ceiling-to-floor room divider is a framework supported by suspension poles. You can either buy the complete unit at a building supply company or just buy the tension rods and make the framework yourself. Either way, they are inexpensive, easy to install, and moveable. There are many ways to decorate this type of frame. You can string yarn through metal eyelets which can be attached to the top and bot-

This colorful ceiling-to-counter divider is made from ball fringe that comes pre-strung on heavy thread and is hung from 1x2-inch strips of wood.

Make this light, airy divider by tacking a semisheer fabric panel to a board on the ceiling and slipping a drapery rod through the bottom casing.

To separate the dining area from the living area, use an inexpensive cardboard folding screen covered with plastic coated, adhesive-backed paper, or fabric or wallpaper.

These dividers can be made from new or used wooden turned spindles which are attached to a three-sectioned wooden frame and then painted with high-gloss enamel.

tom inside edge of the frame. Or, if you'd rather, you can use plastic fishing line instead of yarn. For a really quick and easy treatment of this same frame, you can purchase panels made of plastic, aluminum, hardboard, or machine caning, all in a wide variety of patterns and colors.

Many more materials can be found at second-hand stores and wherever someone is tearing down an old building. Old doors, louvered shutters, and turned wooden spindles from porches and stair railings make interesting room dividers when mounted on a frame. You can also make handsome screens by hinging three or more doors or shutters together.

Make screens of whatever length and width you wish with 1-inch lumber. Fasten the screens together with hinges and finish them with enamel, stain, or antiquing kits. For a more elaborate treatment, add commercial molding or trim and arrange in any design you wish. Screens of

this type are heavy and solid, so you can also decorate them by hanging pictures across one or both sides.

For a lightweight, inexpensive screen, purchase one screen made of cardboard mounted on a wooden frame. You can achieve a limitless number of decorative treatments with these screens. Cover the panels with paint, wallpaper, fabric, pressure-sensitive vinyl-coated paper, menu covers, sheet music, theater programs, record covers, nautical charts, or family photographs.

If you want to make a screen or a room divider, these are only a few of the many possibilities open to you. Choose one of these ideas or use your imagination to come up with a different treatment. But, either way, know how, why, and where you are going to use the screen or room divider, and make certain that the materials and design you use coordinate with the rest of the room's furnishings and decor.

headboards

Does your bedroom look a little blank? Would you like to do something different, yet inexpensive, to your old bedroom furniture? Or, are you still doing without a headboard as you continue to save toward the one that matches the rest of your bedroom furniture?

If you answered yes to any of these questions, there is an easy, inexpensive solution to your problem. Any bedroom can come alive with a decorator's touch simply by adding a dramatic headboard to the bed. And, you don't have to spend a fortune to do it.

Headboards don't have to match the rest of the furniture in the room. There are many inexpensive as well as attractive ones on the market that will go well with any wood finish or furniture style. Try one of the metal headboards in brass or iron. Or, reupholster one of the plastic-covered padded headboards with the same fabric of your bedspread or draperies. Or, you can tour the second-hand shops, basket shops, fabric shops, and building supply companies and come up with a headboard you can make all by yourself.

One of the easiest headboards to make is made by applying panels of fabric or wallpaper directly to the wall behind the bed with double-faced, pressure-sensitive tape. Make it the exact width of the bed and frame the entire panel with colorful, 2-inch wide vinyl-coated tape. To coordinate the room use the same fabric in some other part of the room.

You can have this headboard finished by bedtime if you use quick-drying spray enamel. Attach the drapery poles to a 1x6-inch board the width of the bed, using two screws per pole. Clamp to the bed frame and attach chains to the poles with screw eyes.

This feminine headboard and canopy treatment is perfect for a young girl's room. Purchase an inexpensive wicker headboard and canopy cornice and spray with white lacquer. The pleated valance is part of a sheet and the panels are two twin-sized sheets.

Are you looking for a Spanish headboard? Start looking for old iron fences. First, rework any bent parts back into shape. Next, remove the rust with navel jelly and paint with an enamel made especially for metal. Then, mount to the bed frame.

Make this massive headboard by building a frame and setting in four shutter panels. Cut a piece of plywood to fit inside the frame from below the panels to the floor. Attach dividing strips to plywood, and plywood to frame. Paint and add the fabric.

This inexpensive headboard utilizes a wallpaper border, but in a little different way. The job will be quicker, easier, and less of a mess if you use pre-pasted paper. Draw your design right on the wall and measure accurately to ensure straight lines.

These headboards are made by fastening drapery rods and brackets to the wall. Cut felt strips twice the desired width, seam the edges together, and turn right side out. Loop the strips over the rod and fasten the ends to the wall with mending tape.

inexpensive window ideas

Little touches can create big effects in decorating, especially when they are used to decorate the windows. You can have dramatic window treatments at very little expense if you are resourceful.

First, decide what kind of treatment you want—curtains, draperies, shades, shutters, cornices, valances, or a combination of these elements.

If you decide to use curtains or draperies, you can save at least 50 percent by making them yourself. You can cut the cost even further by shopping for remnants and sale fabrics. Although it is possible to find sizeable remnants at a fraction of their original cost, never allow yourself to be coaxed into purchasing fabric just because the price is drastically reduced. If it's not

To make this dramatic duo, purchase two striped window shades for the windows and one shade five inches wider to cut for the valance. Cut the edging, trim with adhesive fringe, and hang.

Make these colorful frames by stretching fabric tight onto lightweight wood frames. The treatment mounts in the window opening on magnets at the center top. When not in use, the frames hang shutter fashion on hooks alongside the windows.

Re-shape a window by cutting an arch from plywood and fitting it into the top of the window. Paint the arch and the mullions black. Then, antique the shutter panels and window trim. As a finishing touch, use a bright print fabric in the shutters.

Here's a striking example of an easy-to-do window treatment. Make double-fold panels for the inside of the window and cover with yellow patent leather vinyl. Paint the window frame with black enamel. Staple zebra patent leather vinyl to the shade roller.

A wall of glass offers a real challenge to anyone who must decorate on a limited budget. Solve the problem with natural finish match-stick blinds that have been color keyed to the room by weaving yarn through the horizontal slats.

the color, texture, or pattern you need, it's not a bargain, so put it back on the shelf and continue your search. When looking for drapery and curtain fabric, don't overlook one very important resource—the bath and bedding shops of your local department stores. Terry cloth towels make excellent curtains for a steamy bathroom and they're unbelievably easy to make. Wrinkle resistant flat bed sheets, which now come in a fantastic range of colors and patterns can also be used to make inexpensive window treatments.

If you decide to buy ready-made curtains or draperies, shop for stock merchandise rather than custom-made treatments which are always more expensive. Purchase good-quality curtains and draperies, and add your own personal touch—fringe, braid, rickrack, fabric tape, rope tiebacks, appliques, or covered cornices.

Window shades also offer a great opportunity for personal expression. You can buy stock vinyl shades in white or several decorator colors and trim them yourself, using fringe, braid, vinyl and fabric tape, rickrack, stencil and applique designs, wallpaper, and fabric. For further accent, add shade pulls made of large plastic or brass rings, tassels, or yarn pompons. You can also add a matching valance made of shade cloth which can be mounted on a

How do you emphasize a bay window and also use the floor space for arranging furniture? Hang sheers at the window and erect a wall with sheets of filigree hardboard and plain white draperies.

To make a Roman shade, select a firmly woven fabric and cut it three inches wider than the window, allowing 1½-inch side hems. For horizontal pleats, add two inches for each pleat to the length. Use commercial Roman shade tape, and the job is easy.

Let velvety nylon ribbon set the mood for your room. With pressure-sensitive tape apply the ribbon to the vinyl shades. Coordinate the matching table cover and slipcovers with matching heat-sensitive tape carefully applied with a hot iron.

A hand-embroidered crewel fabric is expensive but not when used this way. Rather than bury the crewel work in deep drapery folds, show-case the fabric on wall panels. It takes two-thirds less yardage and gives the room an outstanding center of interest.

Create a coordinated window treatment by selecting a shade with a heat-sensitive adhesive coating and apply a closely woven allover pattern fabric with a hot iron. Hang the shade "reverse-roll." Add a swagged valance in a color picked from the pattern.

Color in large doses will revitalize any window. Make a lambrequin box from ½-inch plywood and cover by stapling fabric around the box. Glue a striped fabric to a ready-made shade. To trim, glue fringe around the arch and across the bottom of the shade.

Bright beads add sparkle to this treatment. Make wood shutter frames from 1x2-inch strips; then paint, hinge, and mount. The easiest way to insert the beads is to buy them mounted on rods. Then, just fasten the rods to the tops and bottoms of the frames.

It doesn't take additional money to repeat a room's theme in the window treatment. To further emphasize this room's south-of-the border mood, it takes colorful fabric laminated to shades, cotton fringe trim, and decorative finial brackets.

To master the ugly radiator problem, distract the eye. Using a vertical design fabric, hang short draperies to the top of the plywood radiator cover. Make a matching scalloped valance suspended by fabric loops from a shiny brass rod.

curtain rod above the shade to create the same effect as an expensive custom-made cornice treatment.

If you are thinking of using shades, you might also consider blinds—bamboo, matchstick, or slat. These can be left plain or decorated, using paint, fringe, braid, yarn, or ribbon, and fabric or vinyl tape. They are very inexpensive, easy to decorate, and are particularly attractive with today's modern furniture.

Fortunately for all of us, the days of the heavily draped and covered windows are over. In fact, if you have ornately carved, dark wooden window casements, no need for privacy, and contemporary furnishings, you may not even want a window treatment. If this fits your needs and the atmosphere of your room's decor, by all means try this "no-treatment" treatment.

Create drapery drama by framing sheer ready-made curtains with side panels made from a 2⅔-yard split length of 48-inch wide fabric. Paint two decorative drapery poles with enamel and hang the panels from a pole at the top and weight them down with another pole through the bottom casing.

If you should re-upholster or slipcover your sofa, buy extra fabric to make a coordinated window treatment. Make matching draperies with pleater tape and hooks. Cover a round wooden drapery rod by cutting the fabric the length of the rod and the width, one inch wider than the rod's diameter.

furniture flair
at a fraction of the cost

There are ways to stretch the dollars you have earmarked for your furniture budget without sacrificing comfort, individuality, and an inviting atmosphere.

First, make a list of all the items you need in order of their importance, and the sources to explore for each. You may need to buy some new and some used pieces that you can alter to fit your needs; and you may acquire some castoffs that can be converted into something distinctive.

If you are shopping for new furniture, look for furniture clearance sales. Sometimes, there are special sales of showroom samples and furniture displayed in model homes or apartments. Occasionally, there are sales of unclaimed freight, post-office sales, and warehouse sales.

Searching for used furniture can be a real adventure, and sometimes produces handsome pieces with true character that can spark your entire decorating scheme. Browse through secondhand stores, thrift stores, antique shops, and visit auctions. Read the want ads in your local weekly newspapers that feature the sale of home furnishings. You will find ads for garage sales, estate sales, people who are relocating and anxious to dispose of their furnishings. Many offices, factories, apartment

For tabletop, cut a 60-inch circle out of a table tennis top; use leftover wood for shelf of serving buffet. Set tabletop on a 2-foot chimney flue liner and support with iron brackets. Cover with laminated plastic.

An unfinished chest was trimmed with stair tread molding around the top and bottom, corner bead molding at corners, and ¼-inch plywood panels at both ends and drawer fronts. After painting, add knobs.

Here, a sturdy picnic table and benches, purchased in a secondhand store, were brought indoors to a family room. They were painted to harmonize with the wall covering and accessories. You might choose to paint the benches a contrasting color instead.

You may not recognize these as standard pieces of unfinished furniture. First, the shelf interior and the drawer frames were painted. Then, the remaining surfaces were covered with adhesive-backed plastic in an exciting and colorful flower design.

buildings, and supermarkets have bulletin boards where people can post notices of items they want to sell.

In your search for inexpensive furniture, look for those items you can rework and those pieces that can serve double-duty. Wicker, willow, and rattan furniture is inexpensive, whether it is new or used. It can be left the natural color, or spray painted a lively color. There are bedsteads, chairs, stools, tables, and bookshelves that can be used indoors or outdoors. Chair and stool cushions can be covered with cotton or vinyl-coated fabric in colorful, dramatic patterns.

Wrought iron furniture, or pieces that combine wrought iron and glass, also fall in the budget class, and still are useful and decorative. Wrought iron can be spray-painted in either a lacquered or metallic finish to harmonize with other furnishings.

Unfinished furniture offers one of the best solutions for furnishings on a budget. You can paint, antique, or finish these pieces; or even cover them with wall cover-

ing, fabric, or adhesive-backed vinyls. If you add sculptured motifs, moldings, and replace the knobs or drawer pulls with decorative hardware, you can create a completely individual piece that can take its place with the most costly furniture.

If you are fortunate enough to acquire an old brass or iron bedstead, even though it may be tarnished, it can be cleaned, buffed, and treated to a new coat of clear lacquer, and be the highlight of your bedroom. An old iron bedstead may look shabby with its dreary gray paint partly chipped off. But, a little sanding and a coat of spray lacquer in a decorator color that harmonizes with bedspread and draperies will produce pleasing results.

You may find sturdy tables that only need refinishing or antiquing. If the top is badly scarred, you can add a wood-grain Formica top or a marble top cut to size and attached with adhesive. If you plan to use it as a cocktail or coffee table, cut the legs off so that the table height is 16½ inches.

ideas for furniture restyling

It is now relatively easy to make old furniture look better than ever or to upgrade new unfinished pieces. In fact, that's why restyling is so popular—it's just easy enough to be interesting!

Also adding to its popularity is the limited amount of time, effort, and expense involved. Money is only a minor ingredient in almost every restyling project and you'll need only a minimum number of tools. Time and effort are easily conserved if you use any of the newly improved finishing techniques now on the market. And, the time you do spend naturally divides itself into short jobs. Space these jobs out over several evenings, if you like.

Restyle an old desk with paint. Using a spray-on antiquing kit, refinish the desk. After it dries, use masking tape to mask off the trim you want to paint. Then, spray the trim and hardware.

Inexpensive pieces of unfinished furniture make the easiest restyling projects. This is because they are sturdy, all pieces are present and accounted for, and there is no old finish to remove. Usually, all that you need to do is add a few strips of molding and finish and replace the hardware.

No matter how simple the new unfinished pieces may be, you will find the most exciting projects in second-hand stores. There are plenty of monstrosities to choose from, but the trick is to know which pieces are candidates for restyling, and which aren't worth the effort. This takes an eye for good design along with a knowledge of what can be done to the piece.

Think first about what you can tear off or cut down to improve the piece. Does the piece need to be changed structurally, or only need the addition of paint and some glaze? Can you take the basic structure and easily add to it to get something useful or decorative? Or, can you salvage moldings, carvings, or whole panels to spice up a plainer, more modern piece of furniture you already have? Often, just some simple re-upholstery will do the trick, along with a new finish.

When considering a restyling project, here are a few things to watch out for: if you can't decide right there in the store what you'd use the piece for or where it would go in your house, you're better off to let it go, no matter how intriguing it may seem. In most cases, without having a definite need, you won't be motivated to get to work, and your prize will spend its days stored away somewhere in the basement. Also, think about how you would go about restyling the piece. Often, when you think about what you want to tear off, you'll see by examination that if you do, you'll be making some structural change that will be difficult to fix. So, in the beginning, choose only those pieces that will be easy to work with. Thoroughly plan each project from start to finish. Know what you're going to do, how you're going to do it, and what you're going to do with the finished product. If you do this, furniture restyling may turn into a useful, relaxing, and satisfying hobby.

A little well-thought-out work with a saw can often turn an ugly, too-high table into a good-looking piece of furniture that is just the right height to complement today's furnishings. Saw off the bun feet and cut away the knobby sections of the legs. After re-assembling, wash the table with liquid sander and give the table two coats of flat black enamel. Next, apply a coat of gray glaze with a "dry brush" technique—dip the brush in the paint and wipe almost dry, then lightly stroke over the table to bring out the highlights. Start with the brush practically dry, adding more until you get the look you like. Cut and cement a piece of black plastic laminate to the top. Finally, tack the chair leg glides to the bottom end of the legs, and the job's done.

how to refinish furniture

During the past few years, the "refinishing" craze has affected nearly every creative homemaker and home handyman, no matter how large or small his or her decorating budget may be.

There are two methods of refinishing, depending on the type of finish you plan to use. If you plan to use a natural or stain finish, you must use the more complex procedure which requires that you strip the old finish down to the bare wood. But, if you want to use one of the many painted or "antiquing" finishes, you can use a simplified refinishing procedure that does not require you to remove the old finish.

HOW TO REMOVE OLD FINISH

Loose joints, splits, or cracks in the wood should be repaired before removing the old finish. After the necessary repairs have been made, brush paint remover generously over the surface. When the finish is soft, dig down to the bare wood with a paint scraper. If all the paint or varnish is not off, apply another coat of the remover.

To remove the finish on curved or carved parts, use a fine bristled steel brush or steel wool. Next, clean off all the remover by rubbing the surface with #1 or #2 steel wool dipped in water. Steel wool holds just the right amount of water for the wash-away type removers and it gives the gentle abrasion needed. When all the old finish is off, rinse the piece with water, wipe it down with a clean cloth, and let it dry completely before sanding.

Sandpaper, steel wool, and shaped sanding blocks will help get your project bare-wood clean and ready for the new finish. Start with coarse paper; finish with finer (at least 6/0) or wipe with a liquid sander and then use a finer paper. Remember to sand with the grain not against it. After sanding, use a vacuum cleaner to get rid of as much sanding dust as possible.

If you've removed the old finish correctly, you're just where you'd be if you were finishing a new wooden piece.

HOW TO APPLY THE NEW FINISH

Now you must decide which type of finish you want to use—clear or painted. The choice depends on the effect you prefer.

If you like the beauty of wood grain, emphasize it with a clear finish. To further emphasize the grain, start with a wiping stain. Wood stains are now available in every wood color, plus many non-wood shades. Choose the color you like best. Read and follow all directions printed on the container. With a soft, clean cloth, put the stain on, then wipe it off. The longer you leave the stain on, the darker the wood will be. Feather and blend the edges so the lap marks won't show.

After the stain is dry, apply the final finishing material. If you want the surface to have a soft-rubbed effect, choose a penetrating sanding sealer. For a higher gloss, use a light coat of varnish. With either finish, apply a light coat, let dry, then sand with #1 steel wool, and dust. Apply a second coat of either the sealer or the varnish, let dry, sand with #0 steel wool, and buff with a soft clean cloth. For a slightly higher gloss and more protection, give the finished surface a thin coat of wax.

If you prefer a painted finish, refinishing with the new "antiquing" kits is quick and easy. The procedure is simple and you don't even have to remove the old finish first. Just wipe on a layer of liquid sander and sand down the rough spots. Apply one or two coats of undercoat paint, let dry, and then paint on a glazing liquid. Finally, try your best to wipe it all off with cheesecloth, stopping only when you get an effect that best pleases you.

You get everything but liquid sander right in the kit. And, a wide choice of colors are available, ranging from delicate pastels to beautiful simulations of real wood grain. Some kits even have spray-on undercoats and glazes that dry in 10 minutes, which means you don't even have to dirty a brush and you can use the piece of furniture the same day.

Use plenty of remover—too little will not take the finish to the bare wood, especially if there are several layers of paint.

The remover has done its job when bubbles appear on the surface. Use a paint scraper to take off the paint and remover residue.

Remove the remaining residue with steel wool pads. Then, rinse with water, wipe it down with a clean cloth, and let it dry.

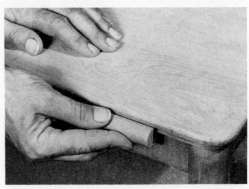

Sandpaper, steel wool, liquid sander, and sanding blocks will help get your project smooth. Dust thoroughly after sanding.

With a soft, clean cloth apply the stain, then wipe it off. The longer you leave it on, the darker the wood will be.

Apply two coats of sanding sealer, varnish, or lacquer. Sand between coats. Next, apply a thin coat of wax for more protection.

special effect wood finishes

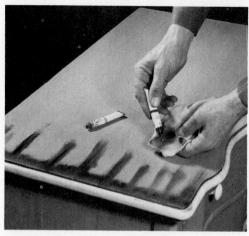

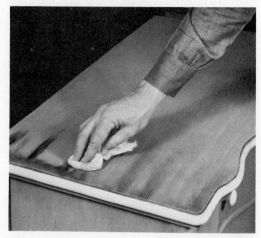

After giving the piece of furniture two coats of flat enamel (glazing mellows colors, so choose one that is brighter than you actually want), make shading and streaks with oil colors at the ends of all flat surfaces. Blend both raw umber and raw sienna on a clean cloth folded into a pad. Apply streaks parallel to the grain.

Feather out shading streaks by wiping from the center of the piece toward the edge. With #1 steel wool, lightly sand the centers of the panels. This will bring out highlights caused by brush strokes in the base coat. Touches like white trim on this chest give an authentic look, but be careful not to overdo the effect.

As a finishing touch, you might splatter the surface with raw umber mixed with oil, using a toothbrush and your thumb to spray on the desired amount. The farther away you hold the brush, the smaller the splatters. After the glaze dries, apply two coats of flat varnish, polish with steel wool, wipe the surface dust free, and wax.

With only a few relaxing hours of work, you can put an antique finish on an old, drab piece of furniture or a new unpainted piece. The materials you need to use are common and inexpensive, the work is simple and fun, and the results can make you feel like a real professional craftsman. Now that you know how it's done, give it a try.

Old trunks abound in attics, used furniture stores, and garage sales. And, the most disreputable of them responds like magic to a paint-and-antiquing treatment. Start by giving it a good cleaning and light sanding. Coat metal fittings with a rust-inhibiting paint. Paint the trunk panels with enamel and apply an antiquing glaze. All of the material for this comes in a kit. To finish, line the inside with colorful wallpaper.

Give any mass-produced piece a look of individuality. First sand the existing finish and cut with benzine. To form an interesting tortoiseshell finish, apply three different shades of any color of your choice. Before applying them, dilute them to a watery consistency with benzine. Let each coat dry thoroughly before applying another. For a subtle gloss, add a clear lacquer topcoat. Spray hardware with enamel.

Liberate a piece of junk and turn it into a useful piece of furniture. This not-quite-antique spool chest started life in a dress factory and almost ended as kindling. After coats of varnish were removed, the chest was painted in a soft gray-blue and antiqued. The glass see-through openings in the drawers were replaced with inserts of yellow caning—sold by the yard for the backing in hi-fi and stereo equipment.

You've probably seen small chests similar to this one in many different shops. With a few restyling tricks, this chest was given a different look. A new top was applied—one with an opening for a copper "sink" to hold plants. After being treated with an overall stain, raw umber right from the tube was rubbed into the corners and cracks to make an authentic looking antique finish. Next, a sealer and then a wax was applied.

Instead of the usual matching table and four chairs, use a high-back settee and trestle table paired with two spindle-back chairs. Coordinate the colors in the antique finishes with hues used throughout the room.

To achieve this rustic effect, use rough-sawed wood. Stain the wood dark, then wash it with a gray glaze. Special antiquing kits with complete instructions make this an easy, timesaving, refinishing job.

Try an unusual finish for unpainted furniture. First, coat the piece with a water-mixed paint base that dries to a texture. Overlap squares of tissue paper using lacquer as glue. Finish with coats of lacquer.

"Cosmetic surgery" can do wonders for an old dresser. First, sand the dresser. Then, give the entire piece a coat of enamel. Next, paint accent colors on the drawer edges, pulls, and carved pieces.

slipcovers

Once, slipcovers were used only when the original upholstery fabric was badly worn or soiled or when the decorating budget couldn't be stretched far enough to replace or to re-upholster the piece. Today, the use of slipcovers is not so limited.

The wise homemaker uses slipcovers for a variety of reasons: to help tone down a room's decor during the hot, summer months, to protect valuable furniture pieces from "peanut butter and jelly fingered" children, and to provide an alternate color scheme for a room.

Many homemakers use slipcovers in the summer months to cool down the mood of their living rooms, when the original upholstery fabric is of warm, sunny colors—perfect for the fall and winter months, but too warm for when the outside temperature rises. By covering the furniture with white, beige, or cool colors during these hot months, the room becomes more comfortable and more serviceable.

As a result of the increased functional use of slipcovers, there is a wider range of colors, patterns, and fabrics from which you can choose when making or buying slipcovers. Another great improvement is in their fit. Many slipcovers are now being made of a stretchy nylon-cotton blend fabric that allows the fabric to mold to the shape of the furniture. You can now find attractive, well-fitting, slipcovers for nearly every style of furniture and at prices nearly everyone can afford.

Despite the availability of ready-made slipcovers, you should not rule out the more expensive custom-made ones. You may not find exactly what you want already made and may prefer to have them custom-made rather than replacing or re-upholstering the piece. If this is the case, get several estimates before you actually ask someone to make them.

Or, if you are a good seamstress, you may want to make them yourself. Choose something simple, take accurate measurements, choose firm, closely woven fabric, cut carefully, fit often, and you will have professional looking slipcovers.

Tired of the same old room? Let slipcovers give it a fresh, new look. A wide selection of ready-made slipcovers now on the market make it possible to change moods as often as the seasons.

build furniture for little or nothing

If you've recently moved to a larger home or are just beginning to collect furniture, you may have a few bare-looking rooms. If so, it is almost impossible to go out and buy all the new furniture you need to fill the additional space. But, with a few handyman skills, a little spare time, and some good ideas, you can build inexpensive "fill-in" furniture that is so attractive it will easily become the central focal point of the entire room.

Look through home furnishings magazines and books, furniture showrooms, and even your neighbors' homes for simple furniture designs. Look for those designs which are made from straight lines and rectangular shapes; these are less complicated to duplicate. Next, when you find a design you particularly like, figure out how you can adapt it to something you can easily build. To do this, mentally break down the piece to discover the construction. For example, if you see a storage cabinet that you like, begin mentally stripping it down. Soon you'll see that it is a rectangular box, open in the front. Figure out how much plywood will be needed to make the top, bottom, back, two sides and the shelves. Next, decide how you want to treat the front. Do you want to enclose it or leave it open? If you want it enclosed, decide on the types of doors you want—hinged or sliding doors of plywood or louvered or panel insert shutters. Once you can see how the piece is constructed, you naturally begin to concentrate on what materials to use. With these two decisions made, you are now ready to go to a building supply company to purchase all the needed materials.

Build an 8-foot hanging buffet for under $60, using ¾-inch walnut-faced plywood for the top and sides, fir plywood for dividers, shelves, bottom, and ready-made louvered doors. Cover plywood edges with wood edging tape. Oil the walnut and paint the doors.

This clay-tile wine rack can be yours for a song. First lay out 5½-inch tiles to determine the frame size. Then, build a box of ¾-inch plywood with a divider in the center and insert the clay tiles.

Fill-up space with an attractive, inexpensive storage unit. Each box is made of ¾-inch plywood 18 inches high and 9 inches deep. Cover the boxes with colorful spray paint and pressure-sensitive paper.

For this entry shelf, find two shelf supports, like these from an old house. Make a plywood shelf, framed with cove molding. Screw shelf to supports and fasten to the wall. Lay a piece of slate on the shelf.

A few 1x10 pine boards make this storage unit that changes to fit your mood and your needs. These switch-around boxes can adapt to any shelving situation. Paint them, stain them, or cover them with plastic.

creative area rugs

Area rugs play an important role in home decorating. Sizes run all the way from three by five feet to room-size rugs; they may provide accent to existing furnishings, or they may be the focal point of a room's decorating scheme. Along with the introduction of new and exciting colors, textures, and designs, there are also new shapes. Ovals, hexagons, octagons, and free-form shapes have joined the more conventional square and circular shapes. They are equally suitable for use over wall-to-wall carpeting; wood, ceramic, or resilient tile floors.

Wherever a bright splash of color is needed, an area rug may be the answer. They can be used in any room of the home, and are especially welcome in front of the fireplace hearth, in an entryway, in front of the sofa, in the center of a conversational grouping, under the dining area table, or beside the bed. The price range is as wide as the choice of colors, textures, patterns, and shapes. But, the ideas here may inspire you to achieve a one-of-a-kind custom-designed rug for a small outlay of cash, energy, and time.

1. One of the best sources is carpet remnants and discontinued samples. These are usually sold at a fraction of the original per-yard cost because they're considered too small to be useful. If you find a remnant 4 by 12 feet, you can cut it into two 4 by 6-foot area rugs, bind the edges and trim with yarn tassels or fringe. For an unusual and colorful area rug, buy an as-

Simple crochet stitches are used for this hexagon-shaped dining area rug and matching chair seat pads. Use rayon and cotton rug yarn and a size 8 hook. When finished, spray undersides with anti-skid compound.

Striped rug is made of two 2½-yard lengths of 30-inch wide heavy-duty awning canvas joined together underneath with a strip of iron-on mending tape. Apply liquid rubber to bottom. Sew cotton fringe to each end.

You can cut carpet samples into interesting sizes and shapes and arrange them to form a strikingly colorful area rug. Combine various weaves and thicknesses to create textural beauty. Shift pieces around until the pattern pleases you, then hand sew them together with heavy-duty thread.

This area rug is made of carpet samples glued to burlap backing. Most of the pieces were dyed. Mix dye solution in a stainless steel or enamel pan and keep it simmering. Wet samples before immersing in the dye bath. Rinse and spin in washing machine. Let dry before cementing to backing.

sortment of carpet samples and cut them with a sharp knife. Glue them with carpet cement to a canvas backing. Let the cement dry overnight, then cut away excess canvas backing. For a bordered area rug, look for a remnant about 6x9 feet for the center, and another 3x9 feet for the border. Cut the border piece into four strips, then cut strips with mitered corners to fit edges of center piece. Glue center piece and border to canvas backing.

2. Fake fur fabrics can also be used to make area rugs. Cut the fabric to size, place a layer of cotton batting between it and the felt base, and topstitch. If you want to simulate the original animal, cut the fur and the felt base in the shape of an animal skin.

3. Bathroom rugs of deep, furry pile are inexpensive and come in a wide range of decorator colors. For a personalized look, use harmonizing colors of yarn to embroider designs, clusters of flowers and leaves, or a monogram. Repeat the same motif on

the matching toilet seat cover.

4. Felt rugs are easy to make and are inexpensive. For greater wearability, use a heavier felt for the rug base (50 percent wool or more works best). Applique felt designs directly to the felt background. If you applique on the sewing machine, set the machine for the full width of satin-stitch and use heavy-duty mercerized thread. If you are doing this by hand, use a whipstitch or a buttonhole stitch. Trim edges with cotton or wool fringe, or a heavy-duty ball fringe. Use a rubber rug or carpet pad under these rugs to make them skidproof, or apply a liquid which is designed for this purpose. Spray with soil-resistant liquid when the rug is completed.

5. If you want to tackle a rug project that requires more dexterity and time, but is well worth the extra effort, there are hooked and rya rug kits available in many sizes, colors, and designs. Each kit contains the base material with the design stamped on it, and sufficient yarn.

storage

There is an old saying, "A place for everything, and everything in its place," that is an everlasting challenge to most homemakers. You may think you've used up every inch of available space in your home, but here are some suggestions that might help you solve your storage problem.

Even if you already have an average amount of closets and built-in cupboards, there are many other storage possibilities. There are shelves and cupboards, both wall-hanging and freestanding. There are room dividers that have storage space. Chests, cabinets, and trunks offer needed storage space. Furniture manufacturers offer a wide selection of multipurpose furniture. Houseware departments carry an extensive line of closet and cupboard organizers that can literally double the storage facilities in your home.

But, before you buy or build extra storage facilities, take an inventory of how much you have. Are you putting it to the best possible use? Could it be better organized? Is it cluttered with items that will never be used again?

ORGANIZE EXISTING STORAGE SPACE

Take a good look at each closet to see what can be done to increase its efficiency. If a closet has just one clothes rod, and one shelf above, there are numerous ways to double its capacity. Start by adding an extra shelf. If part of the hanging space is for men's or children's garments, install another rod halfway down that extends partway across the closet so that there are two tiers of hanging space for shorter length garments. There are closet organizers that you can buy that have shelves, rods, brackets, standards, and hardware. Shelves and rods can be arranged to fit individual needs and can be rearranged, when necessary, as shelves and rods are adjustable. These are simple and quick to install and can be moved if you relocate.

To put up this unit, just drill the holes, tap plastic anchors in them, and screw brackets to wall. Shelves are 12 inches deep.

There are different sizes of see-through plastic storage boxes that have interlocking grooves for non-slip stacking on closet shelves. Less expensive and equally useful are uniform-sized sturdy dress, suit, and shoe cartons that you can accumulate when you buy clothing. Cover these with wallpaper, fabric, or adhesive-backed paper. In closet accessory departments you can find shoe or purse files of heavy gauge vinyl that hang from the closet rod, taking very little rod space. There are also shoe racks that rest on the floor, or ones of tubular steel that slip over the back of a closet door and extend nearly the full length of the door. Hangers that hold several skirts, pairs of slacks, or shirts or blouses vertically also ease crowded closets.

Under-the-bed storage chests of vinyl or hardboard are ideal for storing blankets, bedspreads, linens, or clothing.

STORAGE UNITS YOU CAN BUY

There are shelves, cabinets, cupboards, chests, trunks, and pieces of multipurpose furniture that all contribute storage space. Whether your budget allows you to splurge on an item of fine furniture wood, or if it will permit only the purchase of an unfinished piece, or even a thrift shop or auction offering, you can make your purchase a decorative and useful addition.

In the fine furniture category, there are multipurpose pieces—tables with drawers and cupboards below; wall units with shelves, cupboards, and flip-down desks; cabinets with shelves and drawers; and chests of drawers. Some contemporary designs are made of shiny metal and glass.

Less expensive, but just as practical, are unfinished or wicker storage pieces: unfinished pieces can be antiqued, painted, or given a fine furniture wood finish; wicker pieces can remain the natural color, or be spray-painted in your favorite color.

Chests, cabinets, and shelves that are family hand-me-downs or purchased at thrift shops, secondhand stores, or auctions also can provide good solutions to your storage problems. You can revitalize an outmoded cabinet by treating it to a new finish, lining the inside with wallpaper

Cut shelves from ¾-inch plywood. Seal edges with wood filler and paint. Hang shelves on metal brackets screwed to wall.

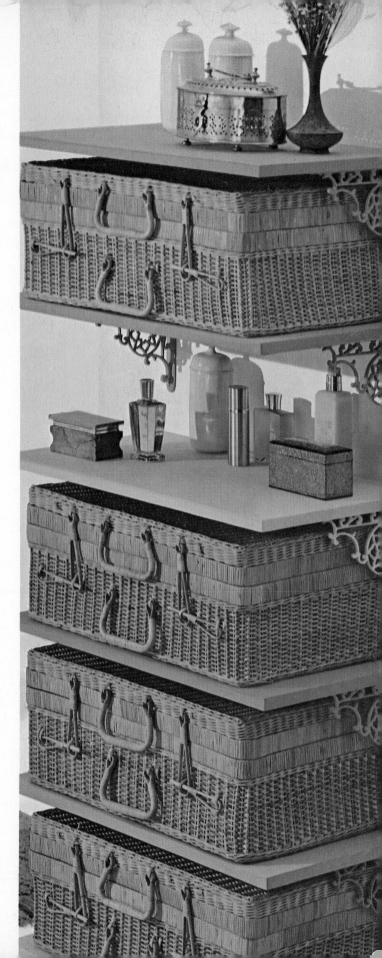

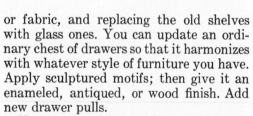

Build boxes of 1x12 boards. Paint and stack them to suit your needs, and add glass shelves. This entire wall unit is mobile.

Build 7-foot high boxes 30 inches wide of 1x2 lumber. Drill holes for shelf supports. Paint, set in place, and anchor tops to wall.

or fabric, and replacing the old shelves with glass ones. You can update an ordinary chest of drawers so that it harmonizes with whatever style of furniture you have. Apply sculptured motifs; then give it an enameled, antiqued, or wood finish. Add new drawer pulls.

You can purchase unfinished hardwood turnings, predrilled shelves, and connectors at local building supply dealers that enable you to assemble any number of shelf arrangements in a matter of minutes. You don't even need any tools or glue; just assemble them by twisting the pieces together and painting, antiquing, or staining them to obtain the desired finish.

There are also shelves supported by suspension poles that can be placed against a wall, or freestanding to act as a divider. This type of installation permits arrangement of a single shelf or series of shelves, a desk unit, or a wall of storage units.

STORAGE UNITS TO BUILD
There are many types of storage units of simple construction that can be built inexpensively by the home handyman.

Shelves are a valuable addition to any room in the home, or in the basement or garage. Boards can be cut to length at the lumberyard and mounted on wall brackets or upright supports.

A deluxe headboard with built-in shelves below the bed solves the extra storage needs of the master bedroom. Very often, the space under the bed does nothing but gather dust. Put this space to work by building a large, shallow box without a top and bolting casters to the bottom. You can slide this in and out easily.

Basement stairway doors are very often narrower than the stairwell. Put this space to work by building a cabinet with hinged and sliding doors for storing mops, brooms, and other cleaning tools.

If you are looking for ways to add storage space in your kitchen, there are inexpensive and convenient solutions.

You can convert a closet into a handy food and utensil keeper by installing cutaway shelves on adjustable shelf strips and brackets. Vary the shelf sizes and shapes to suit the things you'll store. Hang shelves on the inside of the door for small packages and spices, or mount a piece of pegboard with hooks for hanging cleaning gear such as brooms and mops.

Miniature cabinets can be attached to the bottom of the upper cupboards to relieve deeper shelves of small packages, glassware, and spices. Enclose these narrow shelves with sliding doors on nylon tracks to keep items dustproof. Or, you can buy inexpensive spacemaker drawers that attach under the upper cupboards.

Shallow trays can be added to cupboard base units to hold flatware, linens, utensils, and paper goods. You'll still have full use of the shelves below. If items at the rear of the shelves are hard to reach, replace the shelves with similar slide-outs made of $\frac{1}{2}$-inch plywood. You can also buy slide-out racks that hold lids in an upright position, and turntables that revolve smoothly and make hard-to-reach items readily accessible.

If you have only a shallow wall space or a few inches leftover at the end of the counter, put this space to work for you. Adjustable shelves—$5\frac{1}{2}$ inches deep—will store a lot. The shelves can be left open, or you can add doors across the front. Or, use this space to attach a paper bag holder and hooks for utensils, lids, and pans. If none of your cupboards can accommodate serving trays, platters, and wide cookie sheets, build a tilt-out bin—as deep as space allows. Hinge the bin across the bottom for easy access.

A work center on wheels with drawers and sliding trays below for hard-to-store items or small electric appliances is an ideal helper and can be moved easily.

Diversified storage includes components that can be interchanged to fit future needs. Hardboard files for trays fit grooves.

This stock cabinet, 24 inches deep, holds large servers, trays, dishes, and linens. Narrow shelves are adjustable for bulky items.

extra storage for the bathroom

If you want to add storage facilities in your bathroom, and who doesn't, you will find some place where you can add shelves or cupboards if you really look. Regardless of whether you have a generous-sized family bathroom or a tiny powder room, there are possibilities that you may have overlooked. The cost can be kept at a minimum if you buy ready-made stock items, or if there is a handyman in the home who can build shelves and simple cupboards.

For those who own their own homes, the best solution may be to install permanent built-ins. For those who rent apartments or homes, there are freestanding units that can be dismantled easily and moved when it is time to relocate.

If yours is a large bathroom, you have several choices. You could compartment the bathroom—divide it into separate areas, through the use of dividers. Even a 12-inch deep divider provides excellent storage space for smaller items. If you combine shelves and cupboards in the unit, the shelves will be accessible from both sides. The shelves can hold stacks of towels and a few decorative accessories, and the cupboards can hide an extra supply of soap, toilet and facial tissue, and cleaning materials. The divider unit can be a permanent built-in, or it can be supported by adjustable tension poles which can be moved to another room or house.

A custom-built cabinet can provide a generous amount of storage space. This could fill in an entire wall and enable each member of the family to have space for his own bath and grooming necessities.

Use 1x12-inch boards for uprights, and 1x12s for shelves. Buy a cabinet to center over toilet, and a stock door for long cabinet.

Cut five 1x12-inch shelf boards to length. Attach metal shelf standards to wall. Put in shelf brackets and add stained shelves.

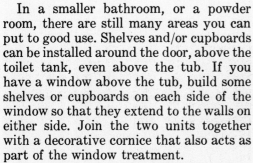

This linen closet utilizes every inch of space. It can be built to fit into an existing closet, or to work as a freestanding unit.

Install metal standards and shelf brackets, then add ½-inch plywood shelves painted a compatible color. Add a few accessories.

In a smaller bathroom, or a powder room, there are still many areas you can put to good use. Shelves and/or cupboards can be installed around the door, above the toilet tank, even above the tub. If you have a window above the tub, build some shelves or cupboards on each side of the window so that they extend to the walls on either side. Join the two units together with a decorative cornice that also acts as part of the window treatment.

If you want to buy ready-made bathroom storage items, there are many styles and types of materials from which to choose. There are shelves and cupboards, either freestanding, or wall mounted, in contemporary, country, or traditional design. They may be made of wood, metal, plastic, Lucite, wicker, or easy-to-care-for laminates. Many of these have matching clothes hampers, waste baskets, tissue dispensers, and towel racks. Some have fine wood finishes, and some have a high gloss lacquer finish. Some are made of sleek, slim strips of shiny metal with glass shelves, others are made of see-through Lucite. Wicker, wrought iron, and unfinished storage items lend themselves to a variety of spray-painted enamel finishes.

If your lavatory bowl is more than a few years old, it may not have a counter with cupboards below. If so, you can buy an inexpensive stock cupboard, or build one tailored to your space limitations. Be sure ready-made units have a plastic laminate top—or apply a mar-resistant surface to do-it-yourself cabinets.

If you have a linen closet that has several inches of space between the door and where shelves begin, this wasted space can be put to good use. Attach several bins such as those used on doors beneath the kitchen sink for cleaning aids. You can use these bins for storing bathroom necessities, cleaning preparations, extra supplies, even children's bath toys.

add a decorator's touch

Your home should have more than a pleasant appearance. It should also have a pleasant feeling—one of welcome, warmth, comfort, and convenience. If you understand the principles and elements of design explained and illustrated throughout this book, your home will reflect good planning and a radiant personality that only you, the decorator, can give it.

At every opportunity, make your home just as distinctively yours as possible. Do this with color, furniture arrangement, accessories, and wall, floor, and window treatments, your tools of expression.

Make a big splash in your bathroom. The room is probably small so you can afford to splurge. Buy some expensive wallpaper or a few strands of beads to dress up the shower curtain.

Color is your biggest decorating asset when adding a touch of individuality to your home. It costs very little (except when purchasing televisions) and it's the quickest, easiest way to express your own personality. Use color boldly and confidently. Don't be timid. Cover one wall in the living room with a vibrantly patterned wallpaper. Or, antique an old cupboard "barn red" to use as a bookcase in your Early American family room.

One of the most immediate ways to express your own individuality is through the use of accessories. Never buy an accessory, not even an ashtray, just because it's the right color for the room. And, display only those things that you really like and those that mean something or do something for you and your moods.

The way you display your accessories is as important as the accessories themselves. For example, if you had twenty-two framed pictures and hung each one on a different wall in your home, no one would pay much attention to them. But if you massed just half of them on one wall, everyone would be attracted to them upon entering the room. For a bit of the whimsical and as a test for your guests, try hanging one of the pictures upside down or sideways in the grouping.

Once you've acquired confidence in yourself as a decorator, flaunt it, and until then, just fake it!

Create unity and additional interest for a good furniture arrangement and a carefully coordinated color scheme by using decorator fabric tape. Apply the trim to the painted screen, using spray adhesive. Next, either by hand or on the machine, sew a matching band of tape along the bottom of a round tablecloth and on sofa pillows. This treatment will require many yards of tape so watch for sales and save.

If you have plain, ordinary windows, you can still have dramatic window treatments. Cut arches from ¾-inch plywood and secure them to the top of four 2x4-inch boards. Cover the inner edge of the verticals and arches with a 3-inch strip of ¼-inch plywood. Then, paint or stain the arches and make color-cued cafe curtains. Install them, using either regular cafe rods and brackets or spring tension cafe rods.

Index